After the Apocalypse

Finding Hope in Organizing

After the Apocalypse

Finding Hope in Organizing

Monika Kostera

Winchester, UK
Washington, USA

JOHN HUNT PUBLISHING

First published by Zero Books, 2020
Zero Books is an imprint of John Hunt Publishing Ltd., No. 3 East St., Alresford,
Hampshire SO24 9EE, UK
office@jhpbooks.com
www.johnhuntpublishing.com
www.zero-books.net

For distributor details and how to order please visit the 'Ordering' section on our website.

Design: Stuart Davies

UK: Printed and bound by CPI Group (UK) Ltd, Croydon, CR0 4YY
US: Printed and bound by Thomson-Shore, 7300 West Joy Road, Dexter, MI 48130

We operate a distinctive and ethical publishing philosophy in
all areas of our business, from our global network of authors to
production and worldwide distribution.

Contents

Monika Kostera

To Zygmunt Bauman – mentor, friend, occasional co-author, whom I had the great privilege of knowing and having the possibility to talk with. He believed that hope is something beyond optimism or pessimism, or, indeed, happiness or lack of it. Whenever I was in serious doubt, I had the immense benefit of turning to him and asking for a word of reflection. I am missing him and these conversations, and so, doing what many authors do when missing conversations with a friend – continue it here, by writing. Only on my side, alas. But, as many writers do, I do hope for an answer, in some form, to come.

Splinters[i]

How could we believe
that what began
with a fratricide
was the golden future
as promised by the billion prophets
of hard work and thrift

How could we think we weren't the keepers
of hills of Sarajevo,
of Athens and Kos,
of the drowned man Jesus

Whatever comes through did not come unannounced
The Muses deserted us
only the Kindly Ones are still
with us

Introduction

The Sociological Apocalypse

In the Delphi museum in Greece there is a remarkable and yet quite ordinary statue which for some reason draws the attention of many visitors, as it has drawn mine. It is known as the Melancholy Roman and it presents a commonplace if very amiable face, with a sad smile and what looks like a shade of tiredness. Or maybe that is due to a 3-day stubble beard. The name of the thus depicted man was probably Titus Quinctius Flamininus, a Roman politician and general who lived from 229 to 174 BC. According to Plutarch's *Parallel Lives*[1], he became known as the Liberator of the Greeks. He held the Hellenes in very high regard and admiration and spoke excellent Greek. He defended the Greeks from Macedon domination and in 196 BC proclaimed the freedom of the Greek states. He also spoke up for the Greeks in Rome, upholding the significance of Greek culture and protecting Greek interests from Roman ambitions. The Greeks respected him in return, minted coins with his portrait and made him patron of several cities[2]. Caught very un-majestically and modestly in the statue, he looks at us across millennia with a remarkably human expression; he could easily be one of us, would the statue suddenly spring to life. I can effortlessly picture him in a toga, as well as in jeans and a hoodie. But what does this ancient man have to do with a book on organizing written in 2019? Well, first of all, the times of Flamininus and these in which we live currently, are not as far apart as the number of years that have passed would suggest. Both his and our times are characterized by profound changes in the way societies and cultures are organized. In his world, Rome was rapidly rising to become the cultural form defining the globe, or most of it. Old and decentralized cultures, such as

1

the Greek, were being pushed back and structurally taken over by more powerful and effective powers. The ways the Greeks have been organizing their societies were becoming obsolete and impossible. And in a then not too distant future there was looming an empire that would, for many centuries, define and control the world. The culture of the Greek cities was in a weak position, stood no chance against much greater odds, in all – was looking pretty much doomed. And yet, it not only survived, but became part of the dominant Roman culture, and continued to live in the remnants and echoes of Rome until this very day. Greek symbols and ideas surround us even now: we look up to Muses, put our faith in Athena's owl, are still in awe of Aphrodite, like to imagine Dionysus and a drinking partner, admire the beauty of Greek style columns in front of our museums (sic) and churches. Without difficulty, we recognize the names of Achilles, of Homer, Aristotle, Sappho. We know what the Athenians did to Socrates, the wisest man in history. Sometimes we hold symposia, use metaphor, some of us are academics, and we still believe in democracy. Something has happened that prevented the dissolution and falling into oblivion of images, symbols and values from that once so endangered culture. I believe that Titus Quinctius Flamininus, one of the less famous characters on the stage of history, was among those who had made that possible. I shall explain why I think so. But first, let me jump to our own times and their state of strange and terrible disrepair.

Zygmunt Bauman[3] used Antonio Gramsci's metaphor of the interregnum to depict the current state of society – in between working systems. The old system is dead and the new has not yet been established. It is a no man's land of conflicting ideas, of sharp polarizations that bring no hope of resolution, as they seem to be all about a choice between one antiquated set of social structures and another, as obsolete. Instead of glorious utopian projects, able to lead humanity forward, to a better project, we are saddled with hopelessness, resulting in us abandoning the future altogether, as seeking ourselves towards a mythical past, that never existed, where all the dreams, that used to belong to utopias, are now located – what Bauman calls *retrotopia*[4].

I propose another, corresponding metaphor to describe what is happening on the meso level of society, which I have dedicated my research to – organizing and organizations. After Karl Weick[5], I understand organization as a pattern forming as an effect of ongoing processes of organizing; the stability of what we call organization is an impression created by persistent sense-giving and sense-making of the participants[6]. The societal interregnum is wreaking havoc – the lack of an overarching social system creates a vacuum, which erodes structures and institutions, which I also regard as patterns created by social processes. Their stability is neither physical nor given. However, they need to be experienced as relatively stable. As James G. March[7] so pertinently pointed out, these are necessary in order for anything to be done collectively, in an organized manner. Structures provide us with roles to play with others and the presupposed, implied rules for playing them together. Institutions are larger, taken-for-granted social patterns, embedded in even larger contexts, thanks to which it is possible to match situations to rules of action with identities and cultural norms[8]. Today structures and institutions crumble and collapse all around us, in all corners of the world, even if not at the same time or with the same intensity. This process involves old and respected institutions, such as the collegium awarding the Nobel Prize, it touches the Catholic Church, wrestling with serious problems, most prominently with the numerous cases of the abuse of children, it plagues the area of politics, where attitudes and statements unthinkable only 30 years ago today define the norm, it affects seriously businesses, which no longer strive to adhere to any other value systems than pure, rabid greed. Liquid modernity is founded on rapidly spreading processes of disconnectedness between social roles, relations, actors, aims and values –

different elements of social structures[9]. The dominant political rationales, neoliberalism and neoconservatism, converge in the de-democratizing effects they have on the political scene, language and attitudes of the citizens, actively destroying values such as the public good and active citizenry, striving to replace them with hierarchic "family" and business value systems[10]. We seem to have become unable to link work with meaningfulness[11], with social good and usefulness[12], even with life itself[13]. The economy has become disconnected from itself, producing a series of irreconcilable crises and drifting into a permanent state of disequilibrium[14], while at the same time invoking the same tired models and concepts such as homo economicus, the economic man, a non-existent and dead entity[15]. Management is divorced from responsibility and executives have become idols and celebrities, deserving of admiration and imitation precisely just because they are high-level managers and rich, regardless of how psychopathic, ungenerous and even ineffective they are[16]. Increasingly even the personal is disconnected from us, as social actors and human agents, as more and more of the personal sphere is outsourced to coaches, caregivers and other paid service providers[17]. The only thing that remains and even grows increasingly interconnected is the global banking system, creating shock waves for the whole planet, such as the 2008 Great Financial Crisis – but the knowledge the bankers held was not connected and so worthless and ignored[18]. All this takes place in the context even more terrifying and universal: of urgent and imminent ecological disaster – catastrophic climate changes and irrevocable harm done to the ecosystem[19].

To depict this state of things I propose the metaphor of the sociological apocalypse. It shows how definitely, simultaneously and irrevocably the social structures are tumbling, "things fall apart"[20] – a sensation that marks most of the meetings, conferences and events I attend, in the role of social scholar or ordinary participant. There is much distress, anxiety and fear in the air and many people speak, metaphorically or not, of The End, looming ultimate chaos or of a loss of meaning and direction to social life. This outcry is of a magnitude I have never witnessed in my life, even though there, of course, always have been doomsday prophets and Millenarianists around. As well as more regular pessimists – a role that many concerned citizens take upon them from time to time. But there is more to the apocalypse than just the destruction and the fear. The Greek word *apokálypsis* literally means "uncovering". The last book of the New Testament, known as the apocalypse, is entitled *Revelation*. This is the second aspect of the metaphor of the sociological apocalypse. As institutions fall, they reveal what is beneath them. The foundation should be based on shared values, but all too often it was held in place by something entirely different: oppression, violence, raw power. In the flying dust and rubble of the collapse, the atrocious truth becomes visible and omnipresent. It is not possible to ignore it, as it literally flies into our faces and gets into our eyes and noses. In the chaos created by the debris it is, however, all too easy to ignore the values. They are there but they are rare and they do not make much noise. They tend to be absent from news. For example, how many, even among the activists of higher education in contemporary Europe, know that Polish academics protested against neoliberal reforms in June 2018? Together with students, they occupied universities in seven major sites of education of the country. Five others organized protests and pickets, and a further two published collegial proclamations of resistance. The banners set up by the protesters pronounced academic values and objected to businessification and appropriation of academia for profit and political gain: "sovereign science", "self-management is our weapon", "free universities instead of knowledge factories", "revolution never sleeps". One of them said: "academia, my love". The protesters organized lectures free for all to attend, touching a large number of academic

5

subjects, from philosophy to organization theory; panels, debates and seminars. The protests joined different people: students, junior and senior academics, trade unions, people from the entire spectrum of politics, including sympathizers of parties that usually do not even speak with each other, with the support of some technical personnel and a few high school students who have applied to university but have not yet been admitted. In one of the occupied university buildings, the floor of the senate conference room was used as a shared space to sleep and protest for students, and academic staff, including a former vice chancellor and a current dean. The ethos and solidarity of these days reminded me of the magical days of the first Solidarity movement, which I recall from my younger days. The feeling of those days has never left me, I think it stayed forever in my bones, which have become attuned to solidarity and hope wherever life takes me. It was happening again, there, in those Polish academic communities. Those values, so precious and powerful, uniting different people, attracted almost anyone who came in contact with them. But not many did. This became a non-news. It did not get into the mainstream media and there are not many sources in the English language which have any report at all of these events,[21] despite some of the protesters' efforts to get their attention. The Guardian, for example, presented several times with a story of the protests, was not interested and did not publish it. For one reason or another, accounts of self-organizing around important foundational values of different communities tend to be ignored by media. Many people are not even aware that events such as the Polish academic protests, or the values that inspire them, exist. Indeed, from my recent conversations I gather that many tend to confuse values with identities. They believe that most organizations, including criminal and predatory ones, have values because they unite people with a particular identity. Identity politics certainly has a role in this – it has become commonplace to place identities where values used to be, as something that forges bonds and that is cherished and should be defended. However, in the institutionalist view, such as that represented by James March[22], values come before identities, which, if they are to become sound underpinnings for structurization, are rooted in more fundamental principles that the organizers are dedicated to. Values demand dedication of attention, faith and life to them, and what singer and poet Patti Smith depicts in her book titled *Devotion*[23]: a profound and generous engagement. Identities are nowadays sometimes presented as given, basic, something we are born with. Because of that they are portrayed as underlying structural elements. However, as it has been argued many times (and also illustrated by contemporary politics),[24] identity divides rather than unites, it does not provide momentum to make connections and form resilient relationships – used this way it even tends to drift into precariousness and become elusive.

In the debris of the tumbling down of structures of the sociological apocalypse, values remain invisible. The oppressive dust is much more obvious and I would not be surprised if, to the average busy and overworked citizen, it represented the one and ultimate truth about society. We live increasingly in a world where we do not feel safe, or even at home, yet so many of us seem to think this is all that there is. As in Margaret Thatcher's famous declaration: *there is no alternative*. And this is exactly what is the most dangerous of today's many perilous tendencies. We need alternatives more than ever, and not just any alternatives but ones which would give us resilient, sustainable and meaningful ways out of the interregnum and into a future worth living in. In the closing words of his last book Zygmunt Bauman gives a severe warning:

> There are no shortcuts leading to a quick, adroit and effortless damming of the "back to" currents – whether to Hobbes, to tribes, to inequality or to the womb…We need to brace

ourselves for a long period marked by more questions than answers and more problems than solutions, as well as for acting in the shadow of finely balanced chances of success and defeat. But in this one case – in opposition to the cases to which Margaret Thatcher used to impute it – the verdict "there is no alternative" will hold fast, with no likelihood of appeal. More than at any other time, we – human inhabitants of the Earth – are in the either/or situation: we face joining either hands, or common graves.[25]

This book is my attempt at an answer to this call. It is one answer among many, a multitude of possible answers. It is based on an organization theorist's radical dissent, a refusal to accept that the dominant order is obvious or normal, or, indeed, one with legitimacy to define the future. It is a useful lens, I believe, in a society labelled over 25 years ago as the society of organizations[26], a tag that in no way has lost relevance today, we are all organizers, with very few exceptions (to whom this book is not directed, of course). And processes of organizing have consequences and reverberations on many levels and in many areas throughout social systems. So, the book's scope is limited to the domain of organizing and organizations, but with possible links towards many other domains and contexts. The aim of the book is to inspire hope, not to define it, explore it or analyze it. It is a way of reaching out into repositories of hopeful ideas and practices that, at the same time, contain seeds of values strong enough to earn the devotion of organizers. Hope has nothing to do with optimism. In his book *Disturbing the Peace*[27], Vaclav Havel says the following about hope:

> Hope, in this deep and powerful sense, is not the same as joy that things are going well, or willingness to invest in enterprises that are obviously headed for early success, but rather an ability to work for something because it is good,

not just because it stands a chance to succeed. The more unpromising the situation in which we demonstrate hope, the deeper that hope is. Hope is not the same thing as optimism. It is not the conviction that something will turn out well, but the certainty that something makes sense, regardless of how it turns out. In short, I think that the deepest and most important form of hope, the only one that can keep us above water and urge us to good works, and the only true source of the breathtaking dimension of the human spirit and its efforts, is something we get, as it were, from "elsewhere". It is also this hope, above all, that gives us the strength to live and continually to try new things, even in conditions that seem as hopeless as ours do, here and now.

Such was also the view of Zygmunt Bauman[28], who believed that hope is, for a social scientist, the desire and also the impulse to make our planet a more hospitable place to live. It is a radical act, because it is immortal, has its roots in the future and needs no proof, which is rooted in the past. It makes life worth living.

And now to return to the modest hero introduced earlier in this text. Titus Quinctius Flamininus, the defender of Greek culture and other Romans like him, who fell in love with the Hellenic spirit and thanks to whom we are to this day divided into followers of Apollo and Dionysus, even though systems have risen and fallen, institutions shattered, beliefs and even religions changed. We do not have priests of either Apollo or Dionysus easy at hand, no rituals to attend, no temples bustling with religious life. But many of us clearly know the difference between the two, present in everyday symbolism as well as in philosophy[29] and cultural anthropology[30]. Flamininus may have been hailed as the defender of Greek cities, but he was not able to guarantee a permanent survival of Greek institutions or social structures, even if he did quite a bit in order to protect their autonomy. In the end what remained turned out to be much more important than the freedom of Greek cities – although undoubtedly it was important for their citizens. The Melancholy Roman saved for us symbols connected to Greek values and ideas. He and his like did that sometimes quite deliberately, but often probably not – the protecting rescue might have been more reminiscent of recycling than heroic rescuing. Classic scholar Inga Grześczak[31] points out how the Romans did not venerate the Greek world from a distance, with the observance of all appropriate Greek rituals and rules of conduct. Rather, they used what they salvaged for their own purposes. As Melvyn Bragg[32] put it,

> The Romans conquered the Greeks, but the Greeks conquered the Romans' imagination.

I believe that much can be achieved by the conquering of imagination and of opening social imagination to be conquered by ideas that bring hope in a good life after the sociological apocalypse[33]. I believe that organization theory has much to offer in this respect. Of course not organization theory exclusively, but as it happens to be the area which I am most familiar with, I propose with this book to bring forward a few good things from its rich repository. We may find it beautiful and useful.

Organizing and organizations

Organizations can be seen as solid institutions, something that *is*, as processes, dynamics, something that *people do*. Both belong together, organizations happen when people act together. Organizations are complicated social phenomena and their existence cannot be manifested in any other simple way. Karl Weick[34] describes this seemingly paradoxical state of things in terms of ever-lasting processes of organizing that combine: "ongoing interdependent actions into sensible sequences that generate sensible outcomes". The results of organizing are like cycles assembling into a loop (but not cause-and-effect chains). Weick differentiates four phases of the organizing process evolving into one cycle. The first phase is *enactment*, consisting of the bracketing[35] of a piece of environment and granting reality to it through actions. The next step is *selection,* when people try to minimize uncertainty behaving according to cognitive schemes. Through that, actions and happenings for some time become a seemingly comprehensible entity. During the third stage of *retention* the outcomes of actions become preserved in the cognitive schemes. And so the process of organizing is both created by the sense-making of the participants and itself helps to make sense of what the participants perceive as real and meaningful[36]. I agree with John Law[37] that it would be best to use the verb organizing more often than the noun organization, which makes us take for granted a false sense of stability and regularity.

Yet, argues John Law, the observation that organizing is steady and can be obsessive is accurate. This is how the process is developing, as a mode of ordering or way of shaping the process of organizing by social actors, which is relatively systematic. In an organization, the strategy of ordering is complex and consists of many co-existing modes that are sometimes entangled in an extremely complicated way. In effect, the strategy of ordering in organizations is hard, if not impossible, to work out. Processes of organizing have many facets, depending on whether they relate to, for instance, a company in the market place and at the same time that of friendship and competition among people, or that of the political game, etc. Moreover, while any of these modes may be generally defined, they all depend on the social actors and the environment they are immersed in. John Law argues that the ambiguity that is typical to processes of organizing is the very reason why it cannot be reduced or brought down to the state of *hideous purity*, as it is unfeasible. Even if that happened, organizing would come to a standstill. The actors participating in the process are complex beings, and no action of any single human can ever be comprehended exclusively in terms of rationality. When people organize, the complexity magnifies. Rationality may be a useful category, but it is irrationality that is the basis for action and change in organizations[38]. And this is by no means the only paradoxical feature of processes of organizing. As Weick points out[39], organizing is about remembering successful outcomes (phase of retention) that broaden collective cognitive schemes, but that at the same time limit possibilities of change – it is a kind of internal compass of how the processes should develop. Barbara Czarniawska-Joerges[40] goes even further to say that, ultimately, organizations are:

> nets of collective action, undertaken in an effort to shape the world and human lives. The contents of the action are meanings and things (artefacts). One net of collective action is distinguishable from another by the kind of meanings and products socially attributed to a given organization.

Organizing depends on meaning making and constant communication which is based on some shared sense of direction rooted in values[41]. This is the stabilizing moment in an otherwise extremely multidirectional and fluid action, and only becomes real when people give it a meaning[42]. This ongoing conversation does not have set boundaries, in fact, they are entirely fluid, depending upon the strategies, the environment and the interconnectedness of organizations in a larger field[43]. This field is defined by a set of dominant binding institutions (i.e. templates of actions and sets of social roles that are taken for granted), characteristic for a specific time and place, stabilizing the social processes of organizing and indicating which activities are coupled with other activities. However, the institutions are social processes as well, albeit more recurring and foundational. Social institutions too depend on sense-making and a set of underpinning shared ideas and values[44]. Many organizations perceive themselves as part of a greater entity: its institutional identity. This is also a process, one of institutional self-identification, connecting the meaning of the own organization with the organizational field that is regarded as representing the most important values at a given point in time[45].

Organizations and institutions change but, under more typical circumstances, they do so in a way that necessitates the least possible change. This is by no means a uniform or straightforward process: Jenny Helin and Marie-Jose Avenier[46] speak of "arresting moments" showing a "stability within change" of social institutions. These moments can, at the same time, give a sense of change, renewal, but also of stability, dependability of the institution and a trust in it having a definite future. Furthermore, organizations tend to change collectively in similar ways, as though they were imitating each other, and they are – institutions make them do so, by providing an image of what is important and what is real. This collective process is known as organizational isomorphism[47].

Management is a particular instance of organizing, when individuals and resources are combined with each other in a coordinated way in order to achieve something as a whole[48]. The coordination may take both individual and collective forms, and there are examples of both individual and team management. According to Sven-Erik Sjöstrand, the starting point for management to emerge is the perceived uncertainty, as management means dealing with uncertainty. Unmanaged organizations also exist, but are not very common. This may be due to the human desire to react to uncertainty in an organized manner, as people often perceive uncertainty as a threat. People cannot predict what will happen and when, but they still have clear expectations that something unexpected will come about – and this is why they want to manage their world. This is an intensive and hopeful interaction with reality; indeed, one can say that organizing and the desire to manage them are collective and physical expressions of human hope.

Stories of hope

A long time ago, in the early 1990s, Poland was undergoing what was then known as "transition" – a forced rapid marketization coupled with privatization of the means of production, aimed at transforming the economy from planned to neoliberal market-based. I belonged to a generation that both hoped for and was ready to take over important posts and reinvent ourselves as a new Western-style middle class. Even though it so happened I went to academia, not business, I saw myself as belonging to the bringers of the future. I did not believe in Thatcherism and was not happy with the ruling ideology, but hoped for a more social-democratic turn of events. Nonetheless, I thought it was we who knew what management was and that the old guard was lacking that knowledge. And so, after my doctorate, I decided to plunge into a study about the future. I intended to interview experienced Polish managers about their visions of the future. I had good access to the field and so I grabbed my newly purchased mini-tape recorder, a notebook and off I went to interview the old-schoolers. They talked, sure they did. They talked a lot. But none, not one, answered my question about the future. Instead they were all telling me stories about the... past. Disheartened and appalled, I phoned my mentor in Sweden. I complained about my field, how they insisted on telling me about the past instead of answering my question about the future. I agonized about my beautiful study, how it was going straight to hell and I asked her for advice. She said:

> You know, you have more luck than reason. You said you wanted to do what? An ethnography about visions of the future? There is no such thing as the future. Ethnography is about real experience. You are lucky, they are telling you

good stuff. Note everything down and concentrate on that instead.

I was baffled but I did as I was told. In the process I began to realize how lucky I, indeed, was. My interviewees were telling me good, important stories about themselves, about management, about what it meant to be a manager in a planned economy and after a while they also started telling me about the present. They never said a word about the future. Neither did I. The study changed my whole world, it shook up my view and my perspective on what management was, who I was, who were my interviewees, what I wanted to learn and from whom. I never looked back. I am still grateful to my interviewees and to my mentor. However, I could not help wondering what if I wanted to learn about the future, after all? If I wanted to do a study about visions of the future, how would I have to proceed? Not ethnography, not survey, it makes no sense of course, but surely there must be a way of exploring…what? Yes, what were the visions of the future? If not real experience then what, unreal? But visions are real, it is just that they are not intersubjectively real. People have visions and dreams and it is as important as being experienced or knowledgeable about something. I realized soon that it was about imagination and there are, of course, good ways of dealing with imagination, which is real, even if not in the intersubjective or rational sense. Even my mentor herself was proposing ways of looking at imaginative realities in her writings about narratives and art[49]. Another influence on my way of thinking about this problem was Professor Heather Höpfl and her ideas of poetics as a way of opening up the space for discourse and imagination[50]. I started to experiment with a method based on these and other ideas and inspirations. I called it the narrative collage[51]. In the beginning, I collected poems on a specific topic from my interviewees, which they wrote expressly for the study. Then I extended the frame to include stories and other artistic expressions as means of performative definitions. And then I switched to stories altogether, still hoping for a poem or two. This is more or less what I do when I engage in studies of the imagination with the help of the narrative collage nowadays. First I shall briefly describe the method and its use for the current text and then I will relate the results of my explorations of some of the ideas of hope that exist in the reality of imagination around me.

The narrative collage is based on the idea that artistic methods are most appropriate to exploring imagination. All human beings have imaginative potential, even if not all actively use it: imagination is a bit like musculature, if unused, it atrophies. Of course, not all are talented artists, just like not everyone can be a graceful athlete, but everyone has creative potential, just like everyone needs at least some physical movement. The collage does not necessarily demand masterpieces as its material. It is an artistic method employed in the visual arts, where fragments of various fabrics, substances or works of other authors, artistic or not – magazine clippings, postcards, images of artwork, pieces of textile, etc – are collected by an artist and put together in a meaningful way. *Coller* means to glue together, and a collage technically does that: it pastes together cut-outs. But there is a more holistic level, where the artistic intervention takes an expression in how the parts are assembled. A composition emerges, and there may be interesting synergetic effects of the fragments. George Braque and Pablo Picasso are often hailed as inventors of this method in the early twentieth century. What they wanted to achieve was transgressing the flatness and the evenness of an image and looking for correspondences between the different parts. They hoped that the viewer would see this but also the whole composition and by being able to grasp the movement between the levels, would be handed a more active role than just that of onlooker, and become invited to co-creation by more explicit sense-making than if she or he was looking at an ordinary painting or a photo.

The narrative collage is a research method of collecting fictive narratives written by a group of interviewees, on a topic given by the researcher and then interpreted on several levels, from the most superficial to underpinning metaphors. Fictive stories are created as a response to or exploration of the domain of the possible, the potential, not yet realized. They can be used for the construction of actual social institutions and structures, or just remain in the sphere of fantasy. Even if there is no direct translating link between the "imagined performatives" and social action, they are important to learn about; the imagination is where our ideas of the future spring from.

The narrative collage is a collective creation, originating with a theme or sentence. The researcher sends out invitations, collects stories and then works with them very much like an active editor, putting together a larger publication from assembled text. But then he or she goes further and uses the material as fragments of a collage, interpreting them, looking for common themes, differences and synergies, and shapes their own narrative, based on the collected material and on their own pursuit of meaning. The text should have a conclusion, it should be a coherent story, but not a closed one: it should invite the reader to think further and create their own metaphor, story or image related to the explored topic. Just like the cubist collage, the narrative collage method seeks to involve the reader in an active sense-making conversation.

The researcher asks interviewees to compose a story on a given topic or beginning with a given phrase[52]. Usually the authors themselves choose genre, create protagonists (other than the ones perhaps indicated in the opening sentence) and construct a plot. The researcher only gives them the first sentence or sentences, leaving the rest of the creative process to the interviewees. Having assembled the material, the researcher edits the stories to fit into a report from the study – a narrative of her or his own. It does not result in any general or local theories about how reality works, but, instead, it is able to throw new light on the cultural context of organizing within the domain of imagination. The way that these ideas connect with organizational reality is through inspiration by touching upon underlying archetypical themes[53] and they thus stir invention and the trying out of ideas.

The stories of the collage may be collected during face-to-face contact or via email or on skype. They can then be analyzed and interpreted in many ways. I have recently come to favour semiotic reading, based on the work of Roman Ingarden[54], who recommends to read texts on several levels of meaning in order to reveal the different layers of symbolism.

I have carried out a narrative collage study as a way of opening this book. I have asked students and researchers from different countries to write short fictive stories beginning with the phrase:

Wow. Planet Earth. Year 2035. My deepest hopes have come true...

I asked the interviewees to choose genre, plot, protagonists and settings. They were welcome to add context, place and detail. In all, I collected 20 stories from different authors: six researchers, eight master students and six doctoral students, from Poland, Australia, Sweden and the UK. Some of the authors signed their narratives, others chose to remain anonymous. I will quote some of the stories more extensively and others less so, not because they were of poor quality or uninteresting – there is much very inventive and well-written material in my collection – but because the collage needs a structure and some of the material ends up more in the forefront, whereas some, while still present, remains in the background. This is how a collage works and narrative collage is not different in its main structure.

My interpretation of the collage is inspired by the

phenomenological reading by Roman Ingarden, looking for levels. I have found three levels relevant for the reading of the collected stories: narration, meaning and underpinning metaphors.

And then there was hope: level of narration

The plot in a story is the movement between stable conditions – the difference between beginning and end. I have suggested a positive outcome by my initial sentences, but not all authors went along with it: some turned the plot around and made the beginning ironic or sinister. All stories, except one, are stories of change, either evolutionary or revolutionary. All stories, except one, also focus on one dimension: global or local of the change. The one exception is a poem, expressing ambivalence and liminality, both in terms of mode and breadth of the change.

Global change

There are several tales presenting revolutionary and global change, such as, for example, in the tale by Alexandra Pitsis:

Wow. Planet Earth. Year 2035. My deepest hopes have come true…

I experience a blissful truth and it is so comforting deep down in the deepest folds of my soul…This *truth is elegant and complex*…Let me share my revelations because they will give you hope, courage and surprise you.

For a long time I believed many things that made me feel dejected about the world, people and our trajectory. I believed I was living in fragile times, breakable and brittle. A time where people looked to leaders in high and low places and all we found was uncertainty, incompetence and at best *good will without substance*.

Life until this point had tested my beliefs severely, *the best of human spirit always overcomes the worst* by innate natural desire and will. Though it seems like an aporia, *the same thing that can save us, shatters us down into pieces.*

So what is this truth that strips away everything? My fears dissolve, shedding my persistent horrors about where things were all going. I'd like to say that there is an order to all this but this is not the case. *Order is not a requirement* for what I experience. Nor is 'meaning' as we understand it.

2035 marks the era when the earth shifts unexpectedly, in a way scientists cannot understand, explain or measure. What occurs is the appearance of portals scattered all over the globe, accessible to all and everything.

This phenomenon slows down the earth and time. Forces of life and nature are manifested to us in a way we find welcoming, to hide its absolute turbulence – the portals strewn everywhere on earth are adorned with a *white door* – on entering the door you are *swallowed up whole and gifted with an unimaginable healing cognition.* An awareness *that is not rationale.*

The earth now nestles you gently – surrounds you the way it always has. Now that you cross this healing threshold, you travel beyond what is deemed "conscience". You are now in the realm of humanity and its senses, intricately tied in with the texture of the world.

The revolutionary moment occurred when there appeared an artefact creating awareness, a door through which people were able to pass, changing their own minds and the surrounding world as well, producing healing to and between the world and humanity.

Tommy Jensen's tale is also of a global character, but here the main shift pertains to the natural environment, of which humans are a part. Learning to live with the ecosystem is also saving humans from disaster.

Wow. Planet Earth. Year 2035. My deepest hopes have come

true, but through disaster. Mother Nature finally protested by allowing the ecosystems to go through radical change, thus confronting us with the bare fact that nature's slogan like resilience (as cleaning lady and as horn of plenty) was indeed a myth. Luckily, it did not throw us back to prehistoric time. The domino-effect were not total, i.e. individual ecosystems affecting other ecosystems to render system collapse. It was close but it stayed at radical change. In a few years the Earth got warmer, much warmer. Weather also got worse, lot worse.

It all began with a refugee crisis of epic proportions, people started to flee *en masse*.

...How did it happen? We don't know. But as a serial killer's deed can give rise to the copycat phenomenon, people started to run, and run together, at numerous places within a very short time span...The marathon lasted for years, but within a couple of months relatively few places on earth became flooded with humans.

Megacities started to rise, potentially dystopian, yet something unexpectedly shifted in the human relationships that arose in them. In fact;

...Earth was not divided into wasteland and megacities. Around the megacities there were water and soil, and it quickly become organized. Farming went back to being the main occupation.

There were wars raging and several areas became bombed and destroyed, there was flooding, natural disasters and chaos. The narrator ponders this:

So, what human character am I since I can write that my

deepest hopes have come true? According to old standards I would come across as a cynic, perhaps, but not for sure, as ruthless. I have a vague memory of old standards, I have to say. My deepest hopes have come true simply because human togetherness are now builtd on three foundations:

Humility towards nature...the continuous rotation of people in power...the eternal condemnation of capitalism and communism.

The new human societies utilize solar power and engage in dialogue, trying to establish global peace. The old society is still haunting the new: some outcasts still threatening the cities, toxic waste left lying around. People are starting to die from this. But:

[n]ot so many yet, so there is still time, or so we believe. Hope. Yes hope.

In a story by an anonymous author a Moon inhabitant called Jahim saves the world from ecological disaster. He is happy and thinks of how happy the humans must be out there. But he wonders for how long "hope will be the food for survival" and cannot find an answer. Another anonymous author writes about people rising up against surveillance.

The story authored by Aneta Morgan also narrates such worldwide change, but here it is part of an evolution, progression along the same routes but with a different aim. Now monitoring technology would benefit the many, not the few.

Wow. Planet Earth. Year 2035. My deepest hopes have come true. Compassion is now recognized as the major factor providing sustainable social and economic development. People are regularly checked for the level of compassion as they used to be checked for cancer or diabetics. Now we know that compassion screenings save thousands of lives each year, so they were established as the necessary test for those applying for managerial positions. Future managers are required to have a certain level of compassion (above 75 points), besides necessary skills, university diplomas, and work experience. Compassion screenings involve testing apparently nice, helpful people for signs of lack of compassion, which can lead to selfish and cruel acts when dealing with subordinates. These tests can save lives by finding lack of compassion at the early stage, before it destroys a whole community by advancing self-interest and self-promotion at the expense of others. The most difficult part was to find a quick and dependable way to measure a level of compassion, similar to blood tests that can measure cholesterol or triglyceride levels in the blood. Now we have such test, it is easy, inexpensive and dependable. It is not a place to get into technical details but taking a test is as simple as measuring blood pressure. But, what is more important, we have found that it is possible to increase the low level of compassion by doing voluntary work for people in need. Those who are not interested in managerial position are not obliged to raise their level of compassion but they are expected to find in a given period of time a suitable self-employment, where they depend mainly on themselves. Those with a compassion level above 95 points are offered positions assisting victims of the previous social and economic system: in reconstructing natural environment and reframing their social milieu.

The global shift towards more humanity is a common thread. Marta Połeć concludes her evolutionary global story, depicting the tendency to even more technology and less contact, on a hopeful note: "How lucky I am to see that we are still humans, still looking into eyes of each other, taking care of our feelings, worries and dreams..." In a tale by Woman (who preferred to be anonymous), Earth is saved by better education. Humans realize that less is better and a new society based on degrowth is founded, just in time to save the world. Kinga's tale presents an Earth where people finally live in peace – a time has come for building relationships and living in the present. Rita Poświatowska's lovely short tale begins with a poetic moment: "two swallows began to make spring in human consciousness" and so humans ended up being human again. It was a slow process, a development, but also a deep desire that has been present at the heart of the world and which started to win over corporate mindlessness, materialism and financial wealth.

Local stories

Several stories present a more local plot which, again, can be either revolutionary or evolutionary. One of the most powerful stories of this kind is outlined by Robert McMurray in his beautiful poem *Brief Encounters*. It is local and portrays at the same time a moment and the core of humanity:

I unfold the black ribbon before me.
Slowly at first.
This is time for me.
Time to breath.
I develop a rhythm.
I gather speed, moving more swiftly as I warm to my task.
Faster still and the tungsten white flecks that measure out the liquorice strand begin to blur.
The works hum and senses buzz.
I press harder, put my shoulder into it, flicking left and then right.
In the moment.
Unforced focus.
Being.

I slow, regather and relax.
People pass by on either side.

We are mutually oblivious – all anonymous characters in each other's scenes.

I turn, arriving at a point at which there is no choice but to try once more.

I measure my effort.

I find my pace, settle, breath.

Progress is study, undisturbed.

Then, a presence.

There is someone behind me.

Close by I sense breath – human and mechanical.

I glance back and see him almost upon me.

"I didn't see you there"

"Don't mind me pal, I'm just catching my breath. I was going to speak in a minute"

He edges closer, obliquely alongside. Similarly attired.

Further engagement required…

"Have you been far?"

"Yes, I set off early. On my way back now. You?"

"Not far"

"I get out as much as I can. Ever since I had pneumonia.

Used to be 15 stone you know, before pneumonia.

I got it twice! First time in summer. Ended up in hospital and nearly died.

Brother found me second time – thought I was a gonner. This was just a few month ago"

"You have had a tough year but look at you now."

The pace slows.

A momentary companionship desired more by one than the other.

The conversation takes an unexpected turn. He talks – he needs to speak, to be heard. I listen.

He tells me how his mother, father, partner and dog all died in

recent years of cancer.
As I listen I cannot help but muse,
how strange and intertwined life strands can be.
Just two days before I learnt of canker within my own brood,
now here a stranger recounts his heartache to me.

And here I listen.
Thrown together by the black ribbon,
sharing the pain of another who arrived unbidden,
I attend in empathetic tone.
I slow my pace once more. My line of flight is not the same as yours.
Time and timing everything. I must wait until the story's end.
"This is me – I turn here"
An exchange of names,
a touch of gloved hands as we flow together, then part.
Along again, oak, sycamore and elm crowd over the
slow flowing molasses.

Now I am pitched downward:
my body gathers pace ahead of me.
Tarmacadam river etched through ancient landscape.
Dappled light and wild garlic scent barely registered by absent
*   pilot.*
Ten, twenty, thirty-five, forty...
Mind still tethered to the whisper of conversation not forgotten.
Body as flotsam. Unheeded current. I am swept toward the edge,
double skinned vulnerability exposed to gradient, grain and gravity.

Where ascending demands
you be in the moment,
descending requires it.
Both promise sweet release and suffering.
The former is written in sweat, sinew, searing breath:
a beautifully arduous labour realised just before the cresting.

To descend is to swim with endorphins, to let go, to flow:
a controlled plummet released in the joy of realised mortality.

Wrenched inward once more: sensing screaming.
Mind, body, machine perceive and work in unison.
Pressure applied, body shifted, limits of adhesion tested
all with a feel of better-late-than-never optimistic foreboding.
Metal screams and flesh tightens in remembrance of contusion.
I shoot the unseen rapids of my own incompetence
No skin torn, or blood spilled,
danger averted – heart thrills.

I pass the ruined Abbey.
Monuments, organisations, empires, people, entire landscapes –
All are fleeting.
Joy, sorrow, pleasure, pain, forgiveness and vengeance –
Fleeting.
Birth, death, health, disease, ecstasy and pain –
Fleeting.
The journey, the encounter, the moment and experience –
Fleeting.

We are ephemerality.
Nothing endures.
There is perhaps some comfort in this,
it is neither good or bad.
It just is.

The poem tells a profoundly human story, even if from the local, individual point of view. The ability to make this connection is hope itself. This makes the plot evolutionary, indeed, evolution is human and humanity evolving, because of this quality.

Irena Barbara Wolska spins a tale of writing a book. It took the narrator 30 years and it is a good thing. Thanks to the book, people will be able to keep the memory of some human fates. Two stories tell about having started an organization: a grass-root organization and a business, making the founder happy but not just on a private plane: both the organizations aim at helping other people. A story by an anonymous author presents the Earth from the point of view of a happy inhabitant of the future where humanity has taken the slow movement into heart and degrowth has saved the environment, life is happy and people finally "look each other in the eyes rather than on some screen".

Marcin Laberschek presents a revolutionary local narrative. Something changed dramatically for the whole planet and it started with one conversation. One in a lone of many. But one which went, if not wrong, then definitely weird.

The university authorities finally decided that the scientific duel between professor Grotowska and professor Strzelecki "On the search for the soul", will take place in the city amphitheater. The interest in the event exceeded all expectations. Tickets sold out in just a few hours.

The clash of scientists was planned for 10:00, but all the seats were taken from early afternoon hours. A crowd of dissatisfied people gathered outside the entrance, but there were no more tickets, so they were not allowed into the premises. They had to satisfy themselves with the TV broadcast or climb the electric poles installed around the amphitheater.

The object of the duel were two different concepts of the soul: professor Grotowska's theory of the multitude of beings and professor Strzelecki's theory of the horizon of kinship. The duel was refereed by the ultimately modern digital parametric system Neuronex 0.4.0. The system's role was to award index points to scientists, to verify results and proclaim a winning concept.

Neuronex: *Please introduce yourselves and present your achievements from the last ten days.*

Professor Grotowska: *Good morning, my name is Danuta Grotowska, I am an employee of the Department of Distributed Beings.*

I have published twelve articles belonging to the research area and seven related ones, including four from the priority list.

Professor Strzelecki: *Good evening, I'm professor Euzebiusz Strzelecki, Department of Internalized Beings. I have published seventeen texts, eight from the parallel list, three from the priority list...And in my spare time I do whatever pleases my soul!*

Neuronex: *I award 25 points to professor Grotowskaand, 22 to Professor Strzelecki and twenty-two, but according to the regulations, I subtract 10 penalty points from professor Strzelecki's credits for bringing up the topic of the soul before the start of the duel. Professor Strzelecki's final result is therefore twelve points.*

Professor Strzelecki: *Oh, for goodness' sake, I did not bring anything up!*

Neuronex: *"Whatever pleases my soul" is a monograph published in 2028 by Andrzej M. Cięciwa from the Department of Hereditary Fibers of the Exact Higher University.*

Professor Strzelecki: *This is absurd. So one cannot even say soul when one feels like it?*

Neuronex: *Ten more penalty points. "One cannot even say soul" is an article from 2019 by...*

Professor Strzelecki: *What bloody nonsense! This literally makes me beside myself.*

And having said that, a second, identical professor Strzelecki appeared next to the original professor Strzelecki.

Neuronex: *Professor Strzelecki, I remind you that all help, including help from other people, is not allowed. I will have to disqualify you.*

Professor Strzelecki (the second): *Wait, this physical imprint of Professor Strzelecki would not help me in any way.*

Professor Strzelecki (the first): *This is a joke...What physical imprint!? Who are you, man?*

Professor Strzelecki (the second): *I am Professor Strzelecki, I am the soul in its pure, identity-defined form of the professor.*

Professor Strzelecki (the first): *What nonsense, it's me who is professor Strzelecki!*

Professor Strzelecki (the second): *No, you are only the professor's monument, the professor as I in the essence of I – that is me. And I intend to win this duel, without you.*

Professor Strzelecki (the first): *You can't win anything!*

Professor Strzelecki (the second): *That's what you think. What can you do to me, you mere container for a YOU without the actual YOU inside.*

Professor Strzelecki (the first): *You think I can't. I can. Since you are my soul, you will cease to exist when I strangle myself!*

... and the body of professor Strzelecki viciously attacked himself, that is the body of professor Strzelecki. Fortunately, nothing happened to any of the professors. The professors Strzelecki (two bodies and a soul) were caught just in time by technical service staff and then disqualified by the system. However, this was the last event in the series of scientific duels. At the end of 2035, the dubious system of metrics was withdrawn and any further use was discouraged by severe punishment. These restrictions affected all universities, as such duels used to be organized everywhere. Unfortunately, professor Strzelecki never merged back into one body: when he acted, he did not think, and when he thought, he could not act. However, professor Grotowska continued her career at the Department for Distributed Beings[55].

A few plots stand out as different. Daniel tells a dark tale, local and private, where the narrator has realized all of his dreams and feels empty inside. He has everything, is thoroughly modern, successful, fulfilled. Everything around him is electronic and high tech. The story ends with the sentence: "I miss you, empty white calendar card with a number on..." Wioleta Gajeska turns the opening of the story into dark irony. The Earth is now a lonely place, nobody talks with another. All contact is limited to technology and things. Humans have fulfilled their dreams but ceased to be human in the process. Or have they ever been..?

Finally, the most enigmatic of them all, the one which is neither global nor local, neither evolutionary nor revolutionary. It is a poem authored by Piotr Jędras. Here it is in my translation from the Polish language of the original:

Wow. Planet Earth. Year 2035.
My deepest hopes have come true…
On planet Earth my hopes
Have dissolved
Wow
Year 2035
On planet Earth hopes
Dissolved
Drip, drip
2035
On planet Earth hopes
Have
Wow drip, drip
On hopes
And drip, drip
Hopes
And…

Slow thinking, sudden leap: level of interpretation

How does the plot in these stories work? How does the transition from beginning to end occur? In the global revolutionary stories, there is physical movement involved. Tommy Jensen writes of a multitude running, a marathon lasting several years. All this movement produces catastrophe but also critical mass, movement of bodies creates space for the movement of souls. Alexandra Pitsis paints a slower picture – in her tale people walk and cross a threshold to be altered and healed. In the anonymous story of Jahim, the Moon dweller who saved the Earth from collapse, the protagonist watches the blue planet from a valley and then, satisfied, slowly walks home to his little cottage. In global evolutionary tales there is also movement but of thought rather than limbs: Marta Połeć's narrator realizes, even in a changing world, that humans are still human. Agata Morgan's story reveals how the now so oppressive monitoring is turned around to serve ordinary people, rather than the elite. Now it is the managers who are constantly monitored, not the rest of the citizens. They have to test positive for compassion:

> These tests can save lives by finding lack of compassion at the early stage, before it destroys a whole community by advancing self-interest and self-promotion at the expense of others.

In this story the act of understanding is followed by physical effort: if the managers fail the test, they "increase the low level of compassion by doing voluntary work for people in need". Likewise the degrowth story by Anonymous depicts first the travel of thought by education and then action and effort to live better and consume less. Meaningful work becomes possible as a result: the narrator is writing her story while sitting in the:

> airplane constructed by the daughter of an ex-worker (you could say: slave) of Zara. I have to admit that I feel very comfortable inside the metal bird, several hundred meters above the Earth. Aviation accidents are exceedingly rare now. And the Earth is slowly regenerating after several decades of abuse.

Rita Poświatowska's story also narrates degrowth and a better, slower life, but the impulse here is poetry. It makes minds and ideas meet, but it is also expressed by movement and by an event: of swallows flying and people greeting each other.

Most of the students' tales – with three exceptions: the swallow story, a short narrative of peace and communion signed Kinga, and a strong albeit brief anonymous tale of people rising up against surveillance – are, interestingly, local ones. Both the narrator's voice and the scope of the presented events are individual or placed within a community, perhaps with some more extended reverberations. Creating an organization is the turning point in two stories. The small business started by Paulina's narrator is about dreams, it helps people to "live in the world which is in accord with their dreams" and this made their lives better. In the second story, the NGO created by the narrator creates a wave of kindness throughout the local community. Action leads to thought. Likewise, in Irena Barbara Wolska's tale the narrator succeeds, at last, in writing a book, completion of which makes her happy, not only because it is an achievement, but because it means that the memory of some people will be preserved. Her slow and persevering work makes something real. This is also present in the other local stories of evolutionary change: thought and action complement each other, albeit in different configurations. In some thought comes first, in others, action does. In Robert McMurray's poem thought and action are closely intertwined. This is a poem about running, or maybe, a poem on the run, but this movement is never purely physical, as it carries thought and communication. The local revolutionary story by Marcin Laberschek is also about thought and action, but here they produce a violent local clash which changes the world for everyone working at a university in the story's world. One of the participants of a "scientific duel" is split in two: a body without a soul and a soulful body which start fighting each other. Even though they never reunite, the happening creates a discontinuity in a strongly divisive social institution: the custom to judge scientists on the basis of their metrical performance. The clash puts an end to that practice: thought and action collaborate to produce a local change, which then has global effects.

It is also interesting to consider the plots which fail to carry the story between the two states, present in most of the stories: a dystopian beginning and a utopian end. There are some narratives where these points are more delicate, as in Robert McMurray's poem: there is a suggestion of an empty space in the beginning and something gained in the end. But in three stories no such transition takes place at all. Piotr Jędrzejas' poem presents a liminality which seems to be both dynamic and timeless at the same time, it is a threshold in itself, perhaps one which needs to be crossed in order to create the movement promised by the initial sentence. Tantalizing but unmanageable, the moment hangs like a drop of water, which ends up falling, but is followed by another and yet another...Finally the two dark stories, where some end is reached but no deliverance in the end, rather, oppression and emptiness. Daniel's narrator has it all and feels unhappy and barren. Modernity is full of things, technology omnipresent and hyperactive around him. He finds himself longing for something long gone: emptiness, the honest emptiness of a blank page of the calendar. Does he dream of a new beginning or of space to think and to act, a space as embodied as he is, despite all the marks of modernity? Wioleta Gajeska's tale is similar in tone, even if not in suggestion of agency. Her narrator longs to see images of a long-gone countryside, with horses, geese, an old lady in a scarf keeping an eye on the livestock. She longs for real images and smells, not mediated by technology. Her ultimate longing transgresses the individual sphere and steps into the natural and the social: she wishes to take away something, just like Daniel's character wants to see an empty page, Wioleta dreams of a society devoid of ambition and of striving for prestige.

Doors and exits: Level of metaphor

On the deepest level, the stories depict a fundamental idea

of hope, what it is and how it works. In the collected stories hope, as a noun, is the utopia on the other side of a door. The utopia is visible and described as more realistic, more liveable than the current state. It has both a human and a natural shape. It is a world where the work of scientists is not measured by competitive indexes (Marcin Laberschek), where humans are just human: ephemeral (Robert McMurray), living in a utopia of togetherness (Tommy Jensen), communicating with each other and feeling for each other (Marta Połeć; neuroza; Rita Poświatowska), reaching for spiritual values and celebrating consciousness (Rita Poświatowska) and peace (Kinga). Humans and the environment are tied together, in accord with the texture of the world (Alexandra Pitsis), sustainable social and economic development is based on compassion (Aneta Morgan), consuming less, living better, employees are treated with respect and dignity (Anonymous), safe from environmental disaster (common thread throughout most stories, most explicitly Tommy Jensen and Anonymous). It is also interesting to see what hope emerges as in the stories where it is not realized. It is something beyond the liminal suspension (Piotr Jędrzejas), a sense of meaningfulness (Daniel), an alternative to the technologized world, perhaps similar to the old-fashioned countryside (Wioleta Gajeska). In one beautiful expression (Anonymous), hope is the "food for survival" and that sums it up really well. The food that nourishes the body thanks to a living planet and the soul thanks to togetherness, and embeddedness in the natural context.

Hope as a verb is, in the stories, a movement: passing through this door, opening, being carried by the force of a poetic moment that perpetually moves bodies and ideas. In several stories, typically the revolutionary ones, when the change is sudden and dramatic, bodies move: run, fly, walk, fight and in the movement the change is realized. In others, usually the evolutionary ones, it is thought that moves, by means of education, insight and consciousness, making hope real. In the narratives where no good state is reached, movement fails to take place, the development is taking place by inertia, the uniform motion of bodies without conscience. One of the stories explicitly talks of portals, white doors that swallow the walker, offering an awareness beyond rationality. Hope is a non-linear transportation, not along the defined main trajectories of development, but into a space found – or not – a crack, as in Leonard Cohen's song, *Anthem:* "there is a crack in everything, that's how the light comes in". The really encouraging thing is that both slow and fast are good ways of reaching and passing through the door. It is there and it has a presence of its own, which is neither a prize to be won or an achievement to be made.

What is it, then? In the collected stories, it stands out more or less literally, is of a non-linear passage through a healing door, unifying body and soul or enabling others to do so, linking the human being to the natural context, the food for body and soul. In the words of the visionary and poet William Blake, the doors of perception:

But first the notion that man has a body distinct from his soul is to be expunged; this I shall do by printing in the infernal method, by corrosives, which in Hell are salutary and medicinal, melting apparent surfaces away, and displaying the infinite which was hid.

If the doors of perception were cleansed everything would appear to man as it is, infinite[56].

The metaphor of the doors strikes a very clear chord with me, too. And as an organization theorist I tend to see the world in terms of organizing and organizations, structures on the meso level, neither great nor small; I have a feeling that I can find and point out some of the doors outlined by others in that level. This is what I want to do in this book. As I said, it is not a treatise on hope. The topic of hope is not even explicitly addressed for the most part of the book. It definitely is *not* about presenting different views on what hope is, their emergence and links to organization theory or practice. In other words, this is not an exegesis of writings on hope. Instead, I will share with the Readers some ideas that can help to open doors and reveal what is hidden from everyday sight.

In the sociological Apocalypse, the process of destruction of structures and institutions, there is also an aspect of revelation of what is lying underneath. Among from the omnipresent debris of violence, there are precious values that have the potential to unite people. Hope opens doors to perception that can enable us to see these values. With this book, I wish to inspire hope and thus help to open some of the doors that lead to organizing and the creation of organizational structures beyond the current sinister outlook due to the Apocalypse of institutions. First, I saw the seeds of hope by reaching out to the margins between organization theory and the reflective sciences: philosophy, sociology and psychology, for a firmer setting in a broader human context. Organizing takes place on the meso level of society – the in-middle area between macro, the grand systems, and micro, the individual. However, it is good to see this place more clearly by the means to sociological and psychological theories and keeping an inquisitive, philosophical mind. In the second part, I make hope grow with the creative spirit of poetics, art and music. Organizations can be closed and oppressive settings but thinking on the boundaries to the arts can help them to be the opposite – liberating and original. Arts encourage complexity and I am a firm believer in the notion that only complexity can save us from simple solutions to complex problems – a common cause to many of today's disastrous economic and social policies. The artistic sphere has an ability to complexify what seems to be simple, to complicate and make multifaceted but at the same time, if approached with the right mind, not too convoluted to be seen or, indeed, grasped. By "growth", I mean becoming more complex, more many-sided, multifarious. The third part proposes daily maintenance for the carefully cultivated hope by the means of powerful narratives: of history, myth and religion. Stories are among the most powerful expressions of human creativity and, at the same time, of our sense-making. In this role they have helped the human ape to create culture and to pass it on to further generations. I have chosen three types of stories from the margins of organization theory: those spinning the historical context, those touching the sublime and the religious ones, with the power of putting structure into the two former types. Finally, in the fourth part, I invite the reader to see hope acquire structure. This can be done with the help of structures that can be found on the boundaries of organization theory and architecture, radical politics and, finally, the very own marginal area of organization studies that is currently rapidly gaining in interest: alternative organizations. From these theories we may learn how to solidify, strengthen and crystalize enough to be able to shatter frames, explode the locks and bolts, to finally throw the doors open towards a world that is waiting after the Apocalypse, that is taking place now. What is behind those doors? I am not sure what to expect. But something valuable will be revealed and preserved for good, future use, after the Apocalypse. That is what Titus Flamininus would do, what he, in fact, did, in his own way, and his own time.

This book is, then, about finding the values and ideas that can help us to sow the seeds of a future we can hope for, make sure that they grow, provide them nourishment and, eventually, see them rise as structures and institutions of a new social reality after the Apocalypse. I propose we do so on the meso-organizational level not because there is none to be found and cared for on other (micro and macro) levels, but because I happen to be an organizational researcher and also because I believe in the power of organizing (I hope what follows in this book can convince you that it is real and strong). The Apocalypse is real: social structures and institutions are, indeed, tumbling and falling. But somewhere among the rubble we can find the values that can unite us and we can look for doors towards possible futures that involve us and the rest of our planet. On the other side, we can plant what we have found, we can do it in an organized manner. But whatever we do, we should keep out of the centre and take to the margins. This is the compass I have been using while writing this book – and I want to share it with you and show where it can lead us.

1. Sow seeds of hope

Philosophy
Thinking hope

For the ancient Greeks, philosophy, or the love of wisdom, was the same as the pursuit of knowledge. Aristotle[57] regarded physics, astronomy and natural sciences – the knowledge of abstract ideas relating to being as well as its concrete manifestations. In his view, philosophy was the ability to perceive and understand the main foundations of what is knowledge. He also divided up this broad discipline into branches such as logic, ethic, rhetorical and natural philosophy. In his view, philosophy is not purely a body of theory, it is also about practice, a way of life. He criticized those who "take refuge in theory and think they are being philosophers and will become good in this way, behaving somewhat like patients who listen attentively to their doctors, but do none of the things they are ordered to do"[58]. Such patients will not get well in their body, and such thinkers will not be well in their soul.

Whereas Newton still considered himself engaging in philosophy, judging from the title of his opus magnus[59], in later time philosophy and science went their separate ways. We have been used to treating the first as purely theoretical, disembodied thinking, while the latter has become a synonym of a factual, concrete and evidence-based pursuit. The divide is often referred, by those considering its origins and consequences, to another great philosopher, René Descartes' famous "I think, therefore I am[60]" published 1637, thus predating Newton. The duality took root slowly and resulted in the almost taken-for-granted divide first in the nineteenth century.

However, some contemporary thinkers, such as Stefan Amsterdamski, whom I had the privilege of knowing personally (if not very well), speak for a return to a broader view of philosophy. In his lectures and books[61] he advocated for the recognition of the philosophical dimension in all knowledge. There is no method, no body of knowledge, no discipline, however empirical it upholds itself to be, which is not founded on reflective, philosophical, indeed, metaphysical understandings. These are sometimes taken for granted, which does not mean that they do not exist. We should become more aware of these philosophical underpinnings of science, Amsterdamski argued. I too believe that this is a good way to regard knowledge and science – as supported and based on philosophy, in a way that at times is impossible, and certainly unfruitful, to tear apart.

The philosopher that comes to my mind first when I think of hope is Immanuel Kant. He was among the first to recognize hope as a very human and complex capacity. For him hope is not merely an emotion, as it was for most of his predecessors, but an ability that can be both rational and moral, indeed, is able to connect the two worlds. In the *Critique of Pure Reason*[62] he posits hope as the faculty by which we relate to what is not, and perhaps even cannot be, experienced directly and thus is one of the fundamental questions of philosophy:

1. What can I know?
2. What ought I to do?
3. What may I hope?[63]

The third question is "at once practical and theoretical"[64], and "all *hoping* is directed towards happiness and is, with regard to practical interests and the law of morality, the same as knowing"[65], presuming one had done what one ought to do. Hoping means knowing that something ought to happen, not necessarily immediately but ultimately and, thus is, real, even if not directly experienced.

A philosophical quest for better organization

Gareth[66] was a management consultant with many years of experience in the down-to-Earth, dog-eat-dog environment of consulting firms, both huge and small. I met him when he was an MBA student at one of the UK universities and we had a chat in the cafeteria after class. He started to tell me about his life, his dreams and hopes and after some time, I asked him if I could take notes for a book I was considering writing and he agreed. He said he was spending much of his life commuting: by train, by plane, by car. That was a time he valued very much, it was purely his own, private time, which he dedicated to reading, or listening to audio books on philosophy. This gave him distance from his everyday world, but was not apart from it, rather, it was something which was much bigger and included both his life as consultant and manager, and his thoughts, hopes and desires for which there too often was no space in the day-to-day work experience. Asked about his favourite philosopher, he answered, without the slightest hesitation, Immanuel Kant. He liked reading and re-reading Kant, never tired of it, because he came closest at seeing and narrating the complexity of the human being, without "going all psychedelic". Humans can be both rational and moral, they are able to solve multifaceted problems on Earth, even if not immediately and not always in a planned, reasoned way. Humanity is not doomed and there is no irresistible force of history or technology which makes everything as predetermined as some management textbooks seem to assume. There is much more to the future than the following of technological trends and obeying market forces. I asked him if he believed that he could somehow use these insights in his work. He laughed and said: sure, even if not by discussing them openly, rather, by being an anonymous Kantian. He was sure there were others just like him. When the time was right, they would be able to shift gears from just muddling through to acting on the big picture which, he knew, existed, even if not in an immediately accessible sense.

Kantian philosophy has been adopted by many, if not mainstream, authors in organization studies, and in particular, in business ethics. One of the most important contemporary researchers adopting this perspective is Norman Bowie, a prolific author, best known perhaps for his fundamental book on business ethics,[67] where he takes up a number of issues, such as why corporations should deal honestly with stakeholders, why it is fundamentally important to make sure that work is meaningful, and that the dignity of all the employees is respected, and how it is the role of business to contribute to the good of society. Now, Bowie is not a radical (and neither is Gareth, the management consultant), he does not call for an overthrow of capitalism and he believes that managerialism is a defensible position, because managers, too, need to preserve their dignity at work. What's more, he thinks that it is justifiable to manage organizations with profit as the main overriding aim, and not, as a more literal adherent of Kant's categorical imperative (such as myself[68]) would uphold, namely, that human beings should never be regarded as a means to any end, including profit and economic growth. Following the latter line of thought, management should be dramatically re-thought and recreated to be aligned with human dignity and human needs, following a profoundly humanistic agenda.

Inspirations from philosophy can be more or less radical, but they bring in perspectives often sorely missing from the profit-obsessed mainstream. Terence Collins and Greg Latemore[69], citing Socrates' well-known aphorism that the unexamined life is not worth living, argue that the workplace all too often is a life unexamined. Philosophy should be urgently brought in to remedy this situation in a methodical way, not just as a way of thinking or as ethics, but as a *practice*.

Historically, philosophers did not after all produce just "theories" about life. Their worldview was also a "way of life". It is this kind of philosophy that we propose managers practise when reflecting on their way of life at work.[70]

This practice starts with not taking worldviews or contexts for granted, with the questioning of one's assumption in order to either accept them consciously or do away with them. Philosophy seen this way is not an academic engagement; rather, it is a way of being in the organizational world, taking part in a good conversation that has been going on for centuries and millennia, in order to understand and interpret. Philosophical reflection is not about dreaming oneself away, but a critical and/or holistic approach to seeing problems and their contexts, which is one of the key elements of learning. Philosophy helps to restore balance in the workplace, the authors proclaim, and in addition it also helps to conquer xenophobia and insularity. People can adopt such a perspective by actively asking themselves key philosophical questions in the workplace, such as: what is real? what can we know? what makes us human? how should we live? who should rule? what is beauty? and: what is our place in the universe?[71] Just keeping these questions in mind helps to broaden horizons and to make oneself more sensitive to the awesomeness of life, but if approached in a systematic fashion, with the help of philosophy, they can have profound strategic implications, for the managers and for their organizations. It opens new ways of seeing and also forges new ways of interaction with the world, ones which cannot be easily foreseen or programmed.

Philosophy can also release us from quite concrete taken-for-granted modes of thought that limit our ability to have insights or find solutions to complex problems. Our times have made rationality one of their fundamental principles. Currently we live in an era of rationality which has become the one and only language available to us, no matter what we do: managers, technicians, academics, teachers and artists – everybody is expected to use the same, reductionist logic in work and increasingly in their private life as well. We have become hyperrational, forcing irreducible human experiences and mysteries into quantitative, even financial, boxes or doing away with them altogether. The image of our times that a – surprised and perhaps repulsed – inhabitant of the future will have, will be one of humans staunchly renouncing their humanity. Is it really so strange that creativity has plummeted these days, if we need to control it, account for it, plan it and sell it? We seem to be in a self-imposed mental prison, of which there is no easy way out. If mystery and creative fury have become unthinkable and belong to the medical or illicit domain, then there is no hope of breaking out by way of sheer human desire. However, there is a way out which can be both presented as rational and which can even be accounted for and planned – the escape from hyperrationality with the help of philosophy of management. A philosophical perspective helps to nuance the understanding of rationality and to introduce a problematization, from a strictly rational standpoint, that opens up the field to new ideas and attitudes[72]. The point of departure should be a consideration of what "sound, defendable view of rationality would be"[73]. Philosophy offers many pertinent views on this issue, proposing that there are many modes and models of rationality. Modes focus on the content whereas models are about ordering and decision-making. Even from this very basic point of view, there are different and legitimate ways of being rational, such as on the one hand, means-end rationality, focusing on choosing the right means for a given end; and, on the other, relational rationality, which involves values. A further consideration reveals even further meanings of rationality, some of which, such as reflective rationality, are very well linked to management science. Scholars such as Argyris and Schön, Weick and Senge, who have been all regarded as key management thinkers, all base their ideas on this type of rationality, derived from Locke's postulate to turn back, inwards, upon thinking itself. Reflection both requires and supports openness, reinforcing wondering, critical ability and systematizing. Having once embarked on this path, thought and action leads away from a narrow reductionist approach and towards what is known in organization theory as double loop learning, that is problematization of the way problems are seen and defined, which enables one to approach complex problems. A good manager, Frits Schipper upholds, should know how and when to adopt the different modes and models of rationality, as they all have a place in organizational practice. Furthermore, the author argues, philosophy may also help to link rationality with feelings, emotions and creativity in an orderly way. Some philosophers discourage us from making such connections but there exist well-respected schools which make them possible and legitimate. Not all types of creativity and rationality go well together, but following the rules proposed by different philosophical traditions may help to find a way to make them work well together. Whichever path is chosen, in organizations reflective rationality should never be absent, as it, in the first place, enables the adoption and adaptation of different modes and models to a given situation.

Another fallacy which dominates management thinking nowadays is materialism. It is often taken for granted as inextricably connected with rationality or assumed to be a distanced, objective approach. Philosophy can help to demonstrate that these options are far from the only possibility for a rational or fair-minded manager. Materialism is just one position and there are many others. Peter Case, Robert French and Peter Simpson[74] demonstrate how contemporary knowledge, or theory, has been derived from the philosophical concept of *theoria*, but having lost in the process some of its key elements: the direct experiential knowledge of the divine. Philosophical practice may help to retrieve this lost meaning, reconstructing management as a spiritual approach to organizing which is neither irrational nor partial or prejudiced. Doing away with the materialist fallacy, which brings about a loss of depth in experience and perspective in thought, is important for managers who wish to understand complexity and approach it at the same time cautiously and constructively, not as an obstacle but as a fact of organizational life to be taken into consideration and perhaps also taken advantage of, in a respectful way. *Theoria* is to be pursued in a more open-ended way that today's instrumental attitude allows for and its quest is directed at the fundamentally unknowable. Such a perspective on management is fully supported by important philosophical traditions, from Aristotle, to St Augustine, to Hadot, and can, with advantage be complemented by relevant organization theories, such as distributed leadership and virtue ethics. Instead of focusing on a narrowly defined knowledge, philosophy may help to acquire wisdom, and especially so the philosophy of the Stoics, argue Peter Case and Jonathan Gosling[75]. The first step would be to reflect philosophically on the lack of wisdom in today's organizations. The next is to deliberately introduce philosophy into the curriculum and re-consider management education so that it ceases to rely solely on reductionist models, stripping ideas and notions from their context. It would also include philosophical practice and spiritual exercises. Stoic spiritual practices included attention to the moment, reflexivity and awareness of the movement of thought. They did not shy away from mystical dimensions of reflection and provided a rigorous and philosophically sound guidance for how exercises should be undertaken.

Stoical spiritual exercises, practices and reflections open the aspirant up to the moment in such a way that they can draw on an unspoken and intuitive well of wisdom; the wisdom of the moment[76].

This path leads to an understanding and awareness of the self which is neither ego-centred nor individualistic. It provides not only solutions and ideas, but solid and practical guidance of how to develop discipline in both thinking and presence in the world. It does so by the three key components of discourse and practice: physics, or the material aspect of the world that cannot be changed at will; ethics or moral action; and logic, or conscious paying attention to thought. These three elements can help managers to more effectively deal with what is the core of their work: the "constant entanglement in causes and effects beyond one's control"[77].

A fallacy related to materialism is fragmentation, a mode of thinking and reasoning disjoined from the larger context. Philosophic practice may be of assistance even with regard to this major problem. Ann Cunliffe[78] argues that managers are taught to think in linear ways of reasoning and offered what is presented as "tools" of the trade. Questioning them is perceived as unnecessary and they often assume that it would be threatening to their career and conflict with doing a good job. She proposes that MBA programmes add philosophical themes of relationalism, ethics and reflexivity to their curricula. Her experience of teaching executive MBA students shows that this is a possible and beneficial approach. Her leadership course focused on teaching the students to think critically and reflexively, which means that they were not offered definitions but, rather, given training in rigorous thinking and relating ideas to experience (and vice versa). They were also taught not to take themselves for granted, but to seek to position themselves in a context, within relationships. The students were presented with a number of philosophical tools and ideas, from Husserl's phenomenology, via Merleau-Ponty's lived experience to Ricoeur's hermeneutical perspective. The students were shown that rejection of essentialism ("there is one way of doing effective leadership") does not necessarily result in relativism or chaos, as they often feared, but could bring much valuable insight and tools for genuine improvement, as the students' comments on the programme show. The central idea of the course, "that if we know *who to be*, then *what to do* falls into place – forms a basis for discussion about how we understand our world, how to *be* in the world, how we bring who we are to what we do, and how we can act in ethical ways"[79], was very well received by most of the students, who had a great understanding that leadership was, in fact, a moral activity. Learning philosophy helped them to develop much needed tools to examine assumptions, consider what is often taken for granted, understand the context and take moral responsibility for being the symbolic centre of an organizational context. In that way, they felt they genuinely had gained an agency to shape the future. And this is currently a matter of greatest urgency, as the natural environment of our planet is being rapidly depleted and destroyed, to the point where the whole Western civilization is more and more often seen as on the brink of collapse[80]. Stephen Allen, Ann Cunliffe and Mark Easterby-Smith[81] argue that a fundamental re-orientation of management education from neoclassicism towards ecocentricism is an urgent need and that this can be done with the help of the introduction of reflexive philosophy into the curriculum. The authors point out that recent studies show that business students are interested and dedicated to acquiring less instrumental and more holistic values. They would like to contribute to a greater good. Philosophy, and especially reflexivity, can help to achieve such a broader and more sustainable perspective. Reflexivity is not the same as reflective practice, which is a down-to-Earth and on-the-spot approach to problem solving.

Reflexivity requires a different ontology to reflection, one in which we situate ourselves in the world as co-creators of the situations in which we find ourselves, by questioning: our assumptions and our role; what we may be saying and not

49

saying; what we may be privileging and taking for granted[82].

Radical reflexivity goes even further, to profoundly re-contextualize human actions and decisions. We are constrained by the many assumptions which first need to be acknowledged and then questioned, and then the thinker-practitioner needs to ask her- or himself, how does the knowledge he or she holds affect the outcomes? What is the connection between what one believes is true and the systemic consequences of one's actions? There is no such thing as "objective business practice", the authors remind us. Value neutrality in management is a dangerous misconception, which has led to the sorry state of today's economy, labour market and natural environment. The exercise of disciplined thinking, guided by philosophical rules and traditions, can help students to reconnect their organizations to a broader context. Managers today are often aware that they have a responsibility for the environment but lack the tools of acting upon that knowledge. Based on a philosophically informed education, they will be able to understand the role of different relationships they engage in but also to reconnect everyday work such as product design or human resource management to a greater sense of purpose.

Finally, philosophical education can help organizers to think more constructively about the future by abolishing the common managerial delusion that change, for its own sake, is an imperative. This misconception is so ubiquitous, that it is shared not just by conservative or neoliberal business leaders, but even by many organizers defining themselves as socialist or communist[83]. And yet change initiatives are largely failures, points out Christopher Grey,[84] tracing the roots of the widespread fetishization of change in management thinking. He invokes the philosophical traditions of the sceptics, as well as some of the thinkers who sometimes are used to support the change fallacy, such as social constructivism, to expose the errors and inconsistencies in the reading of some of the work, as well as other, taken-for-granted, presuppositions. Change has become a "meta-narrative", pervading theorizing and education, not just pertaining to the "flux of the world", which many of the ideas invoked to support these statements claim, but stretching much further, to imply a kind of economico-technological determinism. Change is regarded as an imperative to apply interventions leading in a certain direction. It has become common sense in organizational contexts. It does not mean that change does not occur, but that regarding it as, at the same time, a value in itself, as well as defining it narrowly, is not philosophically sound. It leads to actions and management styles that are neither as effective as they are upheld to be, nor sustainable. The dominant model is mechanistic and it furthers the fantasy of managerial omnipotence. Grey proposes to popularize sceptical thinking in order to debunk such errors of thinking and make them subjects of critical interrogation. Education can help managers to become less susceptible to what often comes instead of sound philosophy, that is – ideology.

I asked organization theorist Stefan Meisek, who has a long and interesting experience with philosophical education in a business school, to share his thoughts about the role of philosophy in management learning. He believes that management education remains sustainable as long as employers are interested in hiring graduates and holding a business school diploma is associated with a career prospect. He thinks that the focus will remain on employability and gaining a first job for the students, not preparing them for a life-long profession. This makes management education more and more superficial and devoid of more profound inquiry, less concerned about students' curiosity and passions. Studying management is becoming a rather dour technical pursuit. Under these circumstances, the introduction of philosophy into the curriculum can serve as a way of providing them with space for pursuing these interests and mediating between the technical and the reflective sides of life. A kind of life line perhaps, or an intermediary between disciplines and modes of relating to the world.

Sociology
Sociological reflection as a way out of the taken for granted

Sociology is a discipline of scholarly inquiry dedicated to the study of society and social relations[85]. Its role is to contribute with a knowledge about humans and their relationships, as well as the larger social contexts that they create, inherit and live it. Sociology, unlike common sense, relies on statements that are derived from reliable scientific examination. It aims at broadening "horizons of understanding, because it is not context with the exclusivity and completeness that comes with any one interpretation"[86]. As a field of knowledge, seeking to grasp patterns and interactions in human society, it has a long tradition and roots that can be traced down to Confucius and Plato. However, regarded as an independent academic discipline, its birth is usually associated with Auguste Comte[87], who first used the word in the first half of the nineteenth century. His ambition for the new discipline was that it would discover the laws ruling society in order to gain a true understanding of how it works. The knowledge could be then applied to construct a better society. He hoped it would develop into a "queen science", that, by the use of "positive science", would become the epitome of human knowing, as it would be able to combine hard, empirical evidence with positivist reasoning and, eventually, methodical policy making. Once the invariable and natural causes of social phenomena are discovered, it will be possible to determine their causes and gain a comprehensive understanding of the properties of the social. Comte's notion of the scientific status of sociology was based on and, in fact, identical with, Newtonian physics. Actually, he initially preferred the term "social physics" to "sociology". However, he was convinced that, by gaining such knowledge, people would acquire genuine agency over how their societies could be shaped and developed. Several of the founding thinkers of sociology, including Émile Durkheim and Herbert Spencer[88], for all their different takes on the subject matter, had similar aspirations for the emerging discipline: to grasp the laws by means of scientific method and then influence the course of development of human society. This agenda became much stronger and more revolutionary with the advent of Karl Marx's monumental project. Marx's famous dictum that thus far, "[t]he philosophers have only interpreted the world, in various ways, the point is to change it"[89], became an encouragement for generations of sociologists who saw their mission as contributing to a greater common good, not for the sake of any "objective progress", but in the interests of concrete social groups and classes, who are suffering oppression, exploitation and discrimination. Marx rejected positivism and focused on, on the one hand, social structures, and, on the other, the real and vital needs of people[90]. Marx's inheritance, as well as other philosophical and sociological inspirations, continues to encourage many sociologists to look for alternatives to ruling systems, as well as for ways of making them possible.

There are two thinkers whom I particularly associate with stepping out of a well-trodden intellectual path in sociological thinking: Charles Wright Mills and Zygmunt Bauman.

C. Wright Mills proposed the idea of "sociological imagination"[91], an ability which makes it possible for the individual human being to rise above his or her social situation. With the use of this faculty, the everyday ceases to seem obvious and lacking of alternative. It allows one to see the sometimes very complex connections between the individual and the historic, societal, and the systemic. For most people, everyday experiences do not help to realize how their situation is embedded in a broader context and how some of their vital problems can be solved on another level. Sociological imagination makes it possible to do so and to learn to understand the links between one's own life story with the place one occupies in society and history. Seeing things from a distance does not mean remaining cool or, indeed, becoming "distanced". Sociological imagination is a contextualization that makes it possible to be passionate, empathetic, engaged. However, the horizon becomes wider and the frontiers defining what is possible to achieve turn less solid. Social facts are always connected to systems and structures, and, whereas the individual may experience them as given and unique, they are part of a larger picture. Sometimes only acting upon the bigger whole, or even beginning in another end that one's own experience is located in, makes it possible to overcome an obstacle or cure a persistent ill. Sociological imagination is what connects us together, it is the stuff that collective experience is made of. It also enables us to grasp the difference between the collective and the individual in a way that helps to focus attention and energy on either, in order to act. Sociological imagination is an ability that has vital individual, cultural, sociological and political consequences.

Zygmunt Bauman was an intellectual giant, whom I have had the great privilege of knowing. He was rather famous for his pessimism and disdain for the easy optimism of some of the advocates of "progress" and "social change". However, a closer look at what he was saying reveals that this is very far from a true meaning of his ideas and beliefs. He used to say that he is a pessimist in the short term, but an optimist in the long and that is the key to most of his writings, especially the liquid modern series and his last book, *Retrotopia*[92]. The latter is a stark and sobering description of a society in which institutions have ceased working, causing much harm and presenting us with a real and imminent danger, "marked by more questions than answers"[93]. It can be said that it is on our ability to use sociological imagination – and Bauman was a great adherent of this notion – that our collective future urgently depends: the book ends with an urgent call to think further than the ostensible current inevitabilities, or else not just we, humans, but the entire planet may come to a sorry end.

Bauman's sociological perspective was sober but rooted in a warm and concerned vision of humanity that, together with a co-author, we have termed sociological compassion[94]. Together with two other key themes: the dynamics of modernity, radical systemic change, it makes up the foundation of Baumanian sociological thought[95]. For Bauman, sociology was a discipline of knowing that brings hope: to understand something is a practical problem it is endeavouring to solve and in this act, it reveals and creates alternatives that we can consider applying. Such knowledge may bring compassionate emancipation. It never was a surprise to me that Zygmunt developed a profound sympathy for the teachings of Pope Francis: they shared a conviction that another social, political and economic world is possible, and that it very much depends on us, humans, if we will, through dialogue, take that possibility and create a viable and better future for ourselves and the planet which we inhabit. His world was not once and for all defined; in his own words:

> If an optimist is someone who believes that we live in the best of all possible worlds, and the pessimist someone who suspects that the optimist may be right, the left places itself in the third camp: that of hope.[96]

I agree very much with David Lyon[97] when he says Bauman's approach to the social is a *sociology of hope,* one which sees "the wrenching realities of the present while simultaneously seeing them as part of the conditions of possibility".[98]

Organizational sociology

The term "organizational sociology" is, to me, very much of

a tautology, as sociology was one of organization theory's parental disciplines (the other being economics) and the two still continue to fuse and mingle: many sociologists, including Zygmunt Bauman, occasionally dabble in organization theory, and vice versa. Also in my life, organization theory arrived almost simultaneously with sociology and with a practical insight, which was, perhaps, the moment of the awakening of my sociological imagination. I was working at a successful small chain of cafes in southern Sweden as part of the so-called "extra" personnel, which, by the way, was most numerous among their workforce. They employed a few professionals: a chef, a cook, a cashier, several unskilled waitresses and a human resources manager. The owners had just come back from the USA where they had been working as managers for a large American café chain. They came back with money and ideas. My workplace was such a managerial direct import, organized according to the, then, latest fashions. It was supposed to be affordable and fun for the clients, and effective and fast for the employees. When I started working, we were four people washing the dishes. When I left a few years later there was just one dishwasher, even though the café drew larger and larger crowds of people. The other places looked pretty much the same – fewer people working increasingly intensively. The owners opened several new locations in a short time. The business was going well, very well indeed. Sometime after I started working there I was admitted as a student of an interdisciplinary organization and management education programme. One of the first courses was organizational sociology. While some of my fellow students complained of how theoretical it was, I was mesmerized – this was a class that really explained what was happening in my world. We read Braverman and Korpi, we were taught about Taylor and Marx (I read the first volume of *Das Kapital* almost in one gulp). This was *relevant*, I felt as if my eyes opened and I saw the big, complicated picture, with the owners, the human resources manager, all the employees and myself, as bits in a big story.

And this is the role that sociology often has in organization studies: of eye opener to a wider societal context and relevance. Martin Parker is one of the authors who have been consistently providing such illuminating insights, who, thanks to his roots in sociology (he identifies himself as "ex-sociologist"[99]), has a perspective enabling him to link two standpoints, the social and the organizational, together in a systematic manner. It is a viewpoint which is characteristic of the British social sciences, where the role of sociology has been diminishing since the 1980s, due to a lack of policy support, and the most vital critical tides it carried have been, instead, incorporated into organization studies via Critical Management Studies. This happened because "organizational behaviour" departments of business schools were in need of a labour force and happily recruited the "overflow sociologists" from other departments[100]. The organizational sociologist was seen as the inheritor of the Industrial Relations school, someone who would be able to make labour even more productive in a "social scientific" way. However, in the 1990s there developed a strong critical school within management studies, entering the field as a sub-discipline, not as a mere tendency or area of interest. This school utilized sociological methods and approaches, as well as many of the sociologists.

Sociology has been bringing in a steady influx of interesting ideas and valid points, some of them belonging to the CMS tradition, some with a less critically defined edge. One of the areas which has benefitted from such insights is the study of organizational structure. For example, Stewart Clegg and Caren Baumeler[101] present the evolutions of structures from Weber's bureaucratic "iron cage", technically rational, focused on stability and efficient use of given resources, albeit limiting human spirit and culture, to the contemporary profoundly fluid constructs, deriving from the state of society which Bauman has metaphorically depicted as "liquid". The authors propose a new view of organizational structure, arguing that the implications of liquid modernity not only touch the sphere of consumption but pervade the sphere of production. Just as Weber's sociological imagination was able to throw light on meanings of organizing in the dawn of the modern management era, so now, in its late phase (or maybe decline), Bauman's thought helps to make sense of a time when individuals are becoming liquid to organizations. This is not just a structuring mechanism but an eroding force, undermining individual well-being as well as organizational continuity, by fragmentation and framing them within disjointed projects.

> Organization no longer persists in any comprehensibly stable way as given forms for any significant period of time; network relationships, premised on contracting and markets, erode stable bureaucracies in both public and private sectors. In organizations oriented to liquidity longer-term thinking and planning will be increasingly surrendered to the moment[102].

This analysis (and others, keeping the broad sociological perspective) shows something that is hidden to many observers of modern life, including mass media: that today, in a time of the seeming omnipresence and omnipotence of organizations, these are, in fact, being undermined at their very core. Contemporary capitalism seems to be devouring (or, more aptly, consuming) itself, bit by bit.

Another area where sociology has been able to bring another level of understanding is organizational power. Much has been written on this topic, and the example I have chosen to present is neither definitive nor representative. I just think it shows very well how gracefully sociology (knowledge on the social macro level) and organizational theory (the meso level) blend and boost each other. An article by Andrew Brown, Martin Kornberger, Stewart Clegg and Chris Carter[103] presents an ethnographic account of a medium-sized architectural firm focused on innovative design. The authors adopted analytical categories from organization studies, such as identity, professionalism and creativity, but looked for wider societal patterns and especially focused on power. The text shows how the meso- and micro-level narratives are effects of power and delineate the dynamics so that cultural assumptions, individual selves and organizational performance are interwoven into a wider dynamics of power construction. This text is not only very informative, but also helps to understand why it is so difficult to organize differently in a given institutional context: power is much more extensive than any organizational structure, identity or ethos. Indeed, "talk about creativity and creative identities does not exist outside of power relations"[104]. It feeds on global cultural capital and on an equally global structure of professional and industrial power.

Belonging is another topic on which a sociological perspective can help in achieving insights which can bring hope of finding new ways of organizing. Martin Parker[105] unravels the tale of the Mafia and the symbolic organizing role played by food. He points out that the Mafia is a business and that the extensive symbolism of community and family that it depends on is a mode of organizing defining inclusion (and exclusion). The Mafia has strong boundaries and an intense sense of internal solidarity. Legal organizations may also try to use similar mechanisms and present themselves as celebrating a "family spirit" or having a "strong corporate culture", but their boundary setting cannot be as strict as the Mafia's, therefore they rely strongly on hypocrisy. The lesson to be learned is that market and family relations do not mix together unproblematically and attempts at blending them result in a number of harms, from pretence to violence. This text shows what organizational belonging *is not* in business organizations. Another study, by Tâna Silva, Miguel

Pina e Cunha, Stewart Clegg, Pedro Neves, Arménio Rego and Ricardo Rodrigues[106], uses sociological analysis to track the social mechanisms that organizations can and sometimes are using to foster belonging. The popular notion of "team spirit" is often used unreflectively by management practitioners and authors, because it is fashionable. What does it, however, mean in structural and cultural terms? The authors carried out a study of a football team and juxtaposed categories and concepts of how the spirit of belonging was being developed, on levels from individual and organizational to social interpretations and constructions. The overarching dimensions revealed a set of deep paradoxes: the paradox of selfless egoism, the paradox of results, the paradox of conflict and the paradox of proximity. This study not only shows an interesting pattern evolving at several levels simultaneously, but shows why it constructs "team spirit" by means of reductionist management: "team spirit refers not only to the individual and collective ability to align opposite, but also to manage complementary tensions".[107]

Finally, sociology may inform the way we see organizational change. For example, Stewart Clegg[108] considers how some of the central themes in Zygmunt Bauman's sociology throw light on changes in organizations and their context. He discusses liquid selves, liquid organizations and liquid aesthetics to understand better the nature of the contours of our changing times.

In a cliché, the reality of liquefying modernity is that the only certainty is change; uncertainty becomes the new norm; instability and insecurity the new order; identity a matter of choice, and choice a matter of improvisational ability and access to the resources available to sustain it.[109]

Individual identities are supposed to replace collectivity, eroding some of the social institutions central for organizing and organizations such as the distinction between public and private, the coherence of self, or the moral concern linked to organizational roles. Without these connections to link responsibility to organizational action, all depends on the individual and his or her capacities, not so much moral as "entrepreneurial" and emotional. Leaders are supposed to foster these capacities in their employees, or, rather, followers, as the legitimacy of managerial roles have now, more than ever before, been tied to charisma and "enthusiasm" in formal organizations. Responsibility, that used to be the very foundation on which management rests, has been outsourced and all but eradicated. At the same time, efficiency is defined as value considered only in costs and profits. The latter do not have to even be connectable to responsibilities, work or, indeed, productivity: it is more than often achieved by tax avoidance and transfer pricing. This all looks very fluid indeed, and fits the so often repeated creed of change being a value and virtue by itself in modern managerial discourses. Organizations look like shape-shifters, project-based, with teams instead of structures, flexible KPIs instead of strategies. However, seen from a wider perspective, they are all but fluctuating. They have become ever more solid strategies for income generation for the elites. The mechanisms allowing for and legitimizing a steady and increasing influx of profit are as stable as ever; more, even, because no other considerations of aims are to be paid attention to any more. In conclusion, Clegg argues that it is necessary for organization theory to engage with sociology, because it enables one to connect with the big questions and big picture, without which the way we understand organizations remains incomplete or even distorted.

I asked a younger colleague and alternative organizer, Joanna Średnicka, why she chose to study sociology. She explained that she originally intended to study law. Just before finishing school, however, she considered a plan B, in case things would not go as she intended. It was at that time she discovered sociology. She got interested if not quite hooked but sufficiently attracted to have a go at the entrance exams. The exams for law and sociology were held in similar topics but the scope was different. For sociology they were much broader and questions touched humanities and art. Candidates were expected to problematize things and think sociologically. She felt invited to take part in something rather than just memorize, as for the law exams. It was also at that time that she came across Merton's book about sociology. And that was what really captivated her mind. "I knew by then that I wanted to find out why things are as they are," she said. So she went for what was initially her Plan B and forgot about law, and never regretted it since. She loved her studies, learning about the different perspectives, each of them interesting by itself, but most of all she liked finding out about their multitude, about the possibility to look at the world using different glasses and seeing different things.

> I can still remember the smell of the classroom, the sounds that the furniture were making, the discussions about the texts and the intensive feeling that nothing ever will be black and white again, that what we see depends on the adopted perspective.

But then she chose management for the doctoral studies. I wondered, why? She said that, when she was finishing her studies, she was tired of being constantly critical and reflective about everything. She longed to do something, stop talking about different possible worlds and start creating a better one around her. She felt an urge to be constructive, try doing something which may be imperfect or not entirely thought through, but that would be a leap of faith, a commitment. She engaged in the creation of an alternative business organization with her colleagues. It felt good but as time went by, she started to miss reflection. And so she decided that she would go back to the university and continue her studies on the doctoral level, only this time it would be something more constructive. Management seemed the obvious choice. Again, the first year held a fascination because it delivered exactly what she was hoping for: practical ideas, models, points about organizational realities. Writing the thesis was presented to the students as a kind of practical project. Which, during the second year, proved to be too much, or, rather, too little for her. Her mind began to drift in all directions at once. She considered quitting. But then, by accident, she stumbled across a book on organizational ethnography and it turned out, for her, to be a kind of illuminating connection of ways of seeing and acting upon the social world: to be reflective and practical at the same time.

Psychology
The force of the human mind

Psychology is the study of the human mind. As a separate academic discipline, it is rather new, but its origins can be traced to ancient Egypt, India, China and Greek philosophers, such as Plato and Aristotle, who often wrote about the soul, the mind and the role of thinking. First in the nineteenth century it emerged as a social science, as the brainchild of Wilhelm Wundt, who established a laboratory dedicated to the study of the mind. In his *Introduction to psychology* he defines the area of the new discipline as dedicated to the investigation of "the facts of consciousness, its combinations and relations, so that it may ultimately discover the laws which govern these relations and combinations"[110]. The definition included memory (as "scope of consciousness") but failed to embrace unconscious phenomena (Wundt rejected them as completely uninteresting), which were later made the special area of interest by psychoanalysis and Sigmund Freud, and then other more or less related schools of thought, such as Carl Gustav Jung's analytical psychology or, more recently, Gordon Lawrence's notion of social dreaming. These perspectives seek to investigate these areas of mind and or soul which are not focused on deliberately, perhaps even unknown, and surface in dreams, uncontrollable desires or by accident, such as in Freudian slips. Psychoanalysis has been criticized for its determinism leading to a fatalistic view on human fates, but insights about the unconscious have also been used for emancipating pursuits, to which we will return in a moment.

There are many other schools of thought in psychology and whereas it is not my intention to outline them all here or to provide a comprehensive overview – my focus is on the story of the paths to hope that I wish to tell, with some more or less extensive digressions, I would like to briefly introduce another perspective, with a different focus. Humanistic psychology rejects the concentration on the unconscious and seeks instead to explore the human potential for development and happiness. Abraham Maslow[111] investigated the steps that need to be taken in order to make it possible for each and every human being to experience genuine satisfaction. He believed that a healthy personality is characterized by unity, coherence and integrity, and that this is the very core of what it means to be human. If only more fundamental needs relating to survival and sociality are met, all human beings are endowed with the gift to be creative, to learn new things, and to be happy.

There are two thinkers I would like to mention, whose psychologic ideas have particularly inspired me to look beyond the obvious in other people and in myself. The first is Carl Gustav Jung, and the second, R.D. Laing. Jung,[112] one of the disciples of Sigmund Freud who went their own intellectual way, regarded the collective unconscious as a spiritual domain connecting all of humanity. Humans are meaning-seeking creatures, and the drive to make sense of life and the surrounding world has always been one of the imperatives for us, perhaps as prominent as the instinct to survive biologically. Perhaps they have existed as long as human kind and "reach back into the mists of time"[113], interpretations change but the images themselves are primordial. The Scottish psychologist Ronald David Laing considered all mental states, including psychosis, as having meaning only within a context. He opposed classifications of people or their behaviours, labelling them as "patients" and "symptoms". People behave in ways that make sense if seen as relationships, processes of communication and states of mind. This sense gets lost when behaviour is slashed up in portions categorized as "disease entities". Together with Aaron Esterson, R.D. Laing[114] recalled and recontexualized conversations of "mentally ill" people not as isolated utterances, but as part of a social setting and what emerged was not only a much more intelligible exchange, but situations far from impossible or closed. In fact, talking with the "mentally ill" revealed many imaginable openings for the way concrete people talk with each other, that is, for the given families, but also for much wider social settings: what we view as normal and abnormal, what is creativity, what to expect from relationships, and much, much more.

Psychological lessons for organizational settings

I met Mats when I was a student of organization theory in Sweden. He was a Buddhist and a psychology student. He was the first person who made me realize that there was much more to psychology than either the detached and not very imaginative study of behaviours, where most of the experiments were carried out on some poor animals or American students, or Freudian psychoanalysis, which I then regarded as sexist and deterministic. Mats introduced me to humanistic psychology, which I immediately loved, even though I regarded it, then, more as a kind of scientific absolution for my being different than an academic discipline. Then he pointed me in the direction of the work of Mihaly Csikszentmihaly, who was then not yet the famous author of *Flow*[115], but a more modest researcher of intrinsic motivation. The notion was an eye opener for me, which helped me to be a reflective critic of modern work, of the kind I had learned through experience and via theories in my sociology classes. Work did not have to be an experience of torment and woe, and work organization did not have to rely on tight discipline and punishment. Humans have a natural desire to work, maybe even a need, good work can be its own reward. Instead of learning "how to make people work hard", I wanted to learn how to "let people work well". Our lecturer in pedagogy turned out to be very open to such propositions and I remember him literally lighting up when I asked him these questions. He dived into Paolo Freire with great enthusiasm and instructed us in the importance of critical consciousness. Yet, he was far from optimistic. In these days it was quite common for teachers to attend students' parties and drink beer together, especially after the exams. So we sat there, in the pub, a few ex-students and the ex-teacher, discussing all sorts of things, when the conversation got around to work and intrinsic motivation. He shook his head sadly and said: "none of this is really possible under capitalism, it's just a dream of a better society".

Which I took then as a let-down but now I tend to see it as an opening, a possibility of thinking up a new world of work, applying psychology and organization theory together. Not just Csikszentmihaly, but many different psychological ideas. I will now briefly reflect on some combinations of the two to show what they can do to the understanding of work and knowledge.

Let me start my musings with some thoughts on motivation, perhaps the most obvious area where organization studies can acquire new perspectives thanks to psychology. A diary study on work-related hope carried out by Else Ouweneel, Pascale Le Blanc, Wilmar Schaufeli and Corine van Wijhe[116] shows that the experience of positive emotions had an effect, albeit indirectly, on how energetic and dedicated to work people felt. The possibility of being hopeful about work had, in other words, an influence on how engaged people felt in their workplace, involving such features as vigour, energy, motivation, effort, feelings of pride and enthusiasm, immersion, and concentration. In other words, it touches both affective and cognitive spheres of experience and has an effect on how things go at work day after day. Hopeful employees achieve their goals to a higher degree and the positive experience accumulates over time. Work engagement is an important form of well-being and has implications for a number of important factors, from individual to organizational outcomes. However, not all about the positive emotions at work is rosy. Psychology may also help to bring insights into the more sinister sides of the "positive" turn in organizational theorizing. Stephen Fineman's article[117] notes that the dominant message seems to concern "cultivating positive emotions in themselves and others, not just as end-states in themselves, but also as a means to achieving individual and organizational transformation and optimal functioning over time"[118]. This looks like a seductive discourse; however, the proponents of conceiving of positivity as panacea forget about the psychological truth that both positive and negative feelings are valid, connected with each other and expressions of adaptation to a given context. They cannot and should not be isolated, and a manipulative approach can bring more long-term harm than benefit. While positiveness certainly can be helpful and appropriate, seen as a good force within the human psyche and an expression of the human need to make sense of our reality, taken out of both social and deeper psychological context, it turns into a deterministic and totalizing image, making it everyone's responsibility to "be positive", no matter what. Furthermore, the separation of negative and positive feelings does not find support in much psychological research. Feelings can be and often are mixed with each other. Dealing with negative emotions is "a core to identity formation"[119], and balancing the dark and the light is a cultural matter and thus important for collective identities. Management programmes, even the more well-intentioned attempts to achieve empowerment at work, are not only bound to fail in many cases, but can produce the opposite of what they aim for: burnout, cynicism and a sense of failure among employees who cannot persuade themselves to be perpetually perky and enthusiastic. The author suggests critical, instead of normative, approaches to emotions at work, making use of constructive doubt and more nuanced theories of personality. Also psychoanalytic approaches can help to acquire more holistic and sustainable perspectives on emotions at work. Yiannis Gabriel[120] proposes to make use of the knowledge offered by these approaches to better understand and integrate the way we deal with emotions at individual, group, and organizational levels. He advocates for a coming together of views stressing cultural factors, such as social constructionism, and psychoanalytic ways of seeing that focus on the conscious and the unconscious workings of the human mind in individual and group settings. It is important not to forget that work organizations often rely on emotional labour – it is expected and required as part of the job. Therefore emotions should be taken into consideration in organization studies, both as a standard organizational product, and as something individuals have to deal with ultimately. There is a human cost of the manipulation of emotions and not everything should be regarded as acceptable. Knowing how emotions work in an organizational context helps not only to deal with them more effectively but to be made more aware of limits and consequences of attempts at controlling them. Emotions are very complex, they have both a socially constructed and a deep psychodynamic side. They cannot be fully disciplined or moulded to fit a desired form and efforts to obliterate them tend to result in suppression with a choked affective side-effect, such as the unconscious sense of guilt. Organizations may both offer hope against negative emotions, such as anxiety, and they may cause a great deal of emotional suffering, some of which appears as side effects or unconscious effects of too much emphasis on rationality. For example, bureaucracies, especially when hierarchical and autocratic, "maintain a continuous level of anxiety"[121], yet, at the same time, bureaucratic settings also produce defences against anxiety. Organizations are indeed "complex mazes in which different emotions travel, mutate, and interact".[122]

Everything that is meaningful is also emotionally charged[123], says Gabriel, so we really need to understand the affective intersections between the cultural and the individual in organizations, or else we will continue blocking emotions to drive peoples' actions, causing strain and suffering where there could be energy and motivation. Another and more recent voice[124] in support of psychoanalytic studies of organizations, confirms the necessity to learn more about affect and emotions in organizations and calls for theoretical inclusivity between the humanities and science, an integration of psychoanalytical insights with social theory and further studies linking psychoanalysis to power and politics. Such a more systematic approach will help to throw light on meaning constructed as affective, imaginary, symbolic, etc.

A unique contribution of psychology to organizational reality concerns dreams and dreaming. Dreams can also be social phenomena and learning more about them helps us to understand collective imagination and the potential for the future. Jonathan Gosling and Peter Case[125] muse on the socio-psychological consequences of climate change, which, having reached a critical point, causes many local rationalities to crumble and present a serious threat to meaning making. Social dreaming techniques may help us to see beyond the crisis, as they offer a first necessary step towards the hope of acquiring a remedy: by imagining the (catastrophic) future. The social dreaming matrix is a method for integrative visioning to be used in community or organizational settings. People come together to report their dreams, which are interpreted socially, rather than individually. It helps to draw upon resources which are less dependent on rationality and cultural norms.

Another key issue that can be better clarified thanks to psychological insight is the phenomenon of leadership, always a great hit in organization studies and recently perhaps even more so. First of all, why "must" everyone be a leader nowadays, when a manager or administrator would have done the job? And why, if good leadership is so celebrated, do we still seem to have an abundance of sociopaths and tyrants in managerial positions? An article by Manfred Kets de Vries[126] presents the problem from a psychological and historical perspective, bringing forward how the following aspects meet in a destructive albeit effective combination: ideology, mind-control, the illusion of solidarity and the search for scapegoats. Humans seem to be holding a psychological makeup that makes it likely to produce "untold numbers of tyrants in the making among us, who will be revealed if and when the opportunity for power arises"[127]. Knowing oneself is both important and urgent, as is knowing the mechanisms of society and organizing. All leaders are susceptible to the dark side, there are no blessed exceptions, because we are all human and not saints. Even the most enlightened leaders:

> are not exempt from the pull of psychological regression... Power and reason cannot coexist peacefully, and reason is always the loser.[128]

Knowing how power works – blurring senses, triggering paranoia, corrupting, helps organizations and societies to guard themselves against its excesses by building structures and institutions that can serve as checks and balances against the abuse of power. According to Kets de Vries there is no ultimate of perfect insurance against it, but structures combined with awareness of one's own demons are the only things that can help us to prevent the misery of tyrannical leadership.

Finally, psychological insights may help us to understand an area that is profoundly undertheorized and marginalized in managerial education – death and organizational collapse. Burkard Sievers[129] uses a psychoanalytic perspective to bring knowledge about this topic, arguing that contemporary organizations, and especially work organizations, fail spectacularly when it comes to confronting mortality in any guise. They not only seem to make a taboo of the topic, but purposefully and consistently prevent people from taking mortality into consideration. This causes a loss of meaning and a falsification of organizing itself. Denying death will not efface them; on the contrary, it takes root in the unconscious, driving a strongly destructive dynamic. Organizations develop a mythology of immortality that fails to offer hope of redemption; it is a substitute mythology, denying mortality and proposing that immortality is available to organizations and, through them, to humans taking part in them, but only if this remains unreflected, unspoken of, acted out *as if* it was obvious and real. Such depersonalized and unfelt survival becomes the ambition of managers and employees, a kind of mindless and soulless collective symbolic incarnation. People symbolically merge to create one collective super-person to whom they entrust their immortality. Making conscious, for example, through psychological insight, immediately makes the illusion crumble – and emancipates the soul, even if it does so at the price of uncertainty and doubt.

I asked Andrzej Jankowicz, a colleague and friend, one of the founding figures of the PCP school in business studies, or personal construct psychology, to share his reflections on what psychology (PCP) can bring to our understanding of organizations. He answered with the following short essay (my questions italicized):

A.D. Jankowicz: An approach from Personal Construct Theory

What can PCP bring to our understanding of organizations?
An organization differs from a collection of people because the people involved stand in distinct and different roles in relation to one another. The people interact towards the achievement of an overarching goal; however, these roles have objectives that differ, to a greater or lesser extent, since they offer different contributions towards the overall goal, contributions that stem from different forms of expertise. And, to the extent that the people involved care about what they are doing, and about their own expertise, they will have different stakeholdings in the overall goal. Consequently, as they interact, disagreements are likely to arise, and these disagreements are not resolved on the basis of who is correct or incorrect – right or wrong – but through negotiation based on the recognition, legitimisation, and toleration, to a greater or lesser extent, of the plurality of these stakeholdings.

Given this unremarkable description of organisational life, it is surprising that Kelly's last corollary, the Sociality Corollary, is not better known in organisational studies. "To the extent that one person construes the construction process of another, he may play a role in a social process involving the other person"[130]. In other words, we enter into effective role relationships with other people (for example, boss-subordinate; line manager-service specialist; marketing-production-finance functional department members) to the extent that we are aware of, and can understand, the other person's constructs.

What Kelly is highlighting is that effective interaction does not depend on construing events in the same way; it depends on knowing how the other person makes sense of the events, *regardless* of how we ourselves see them. The better our Sociality, the more effective we can be in negotiating our way through disagreements about the overall task and how these might be resolved; shelved – or, *faute de mieux*, more or less tolerated (albeit with some insight into how best to live with the consequences).

Does it open our minds to something about organizing that we need to know in order to be better at it? Indeed it does. Kelly's discussion of the Sociality process is based on a view of 'role' that is complementary to the standard Parsonian definition – behaviour based on others' expectations of one's own behaviour – which is the default perspective in organization studies. Looked at from the perspective of the role sender, it is not a 'laying on' of one's own expectations on the other, but its opposite: an understanding of the other's expectations based on a deep knowledge of the other's perspective, the better to *anticipate* their behaviour. Kelly offers a dramatic image: "In idiomatic language, a role is a position one can play on a certain team without even waiting for the signals"[131].

It also emphasizes that roles are not fixed, locked into place by relatively enduring expectations as the Parsonian definition might imply. The more I seek to understand other people's construing, the more I realise the potential variety of sense-making about our shared overall task (whether I share it or not – that's the point).

I can ignore, or I can experiment and perhaps choose. And that offers us a value pertaining to our role in an organisation, offering a direction for personal growth which separates self from role. Mair expressed it rather beautifully. Each of us, he said, is "made up of many voices, a community of varying conversational practices, conventions of discourse, manners of being...many of us suppress most of the voices we could speak with and lose track of the many possibilities we could become"[132].

One more conversation about psychology and organizing

I also had a chat with a younger colleague, Dorota Bourne, once a doctoral student whom Andrzej and I supervised together: he, mainly the psychological aspects, and myself, the ethnographic. She was doing a longitudinal study of a car manufacturing company with multiple locations around the globe, which once used to be managed from the UK, but at the time she embarked on the second phase of her study, its British factories were being shut down. She used PCP to gain an understanding about how the interviewees saw the world themselves, what it looked like from their perspective:

I have always been drawn to psychology probably because of its focus on an individual and the lens through which we can really get close to the person and what makes them tick. The lessons from psychology, in particular Personal Construct Psychology (PCP), had a profound impact on me as a person, how I live my life and naturally how I "live" my work.

Several years into my journey through the PCP field, I had my "aha" moment. It was a moment of deep, almost visceral feeling and understanding that really all people on this planet have such strong subjective ways of functioning and sense making, so different from one another, but what is common for us all is that we all do our best, in psychological terms. Our best with what we have, what we know, what we've been through. PCP calls this individual construing of the world that surrounds us. Other thinkers and physiologists gave this their own labels and names. But what was so profound to me about this realisation is that there really is no place in our world for judgement. This is not to say that I reject all rules, norms and suddenly everything is acceptable. Not at all. But this perspective is the only one that truly enables me, or us, to engage with people's actions in a meaningful way.[133]

What she learned then made a huge difference to her understanding of both her research and teaching:

This simple yet powerful guiding thought transformed the way I teach and think about organisations and management.

Starting from teaching, I shifted my focus onto my students by trying to understand them as individuals who ultimately are doing their best in navigating the maze of adolescent or adult life and higher education. I used to think of my classes as a function of my work where I create some space and platform to connect my research to practice and make it accessible for the students. I still do that but my starting point is now very much with my audience. I imagine what it is that they want, need, do and do not understand and put my teaching plan and content in that context. Curriculum requirements and plan comes secondary as the focus is always on the student. I relate to them differently when I lecture. I talk to them almost individually and openly say how I selected the material for them and how it fits into what I think should work with them. I enjoy my teaching more, I connect with them better and I know they connect better with me. They often comment how different my teaching style is and how unusual it is for them to be asked questions which are simply aimed at getting to know them.

As for my understanding of organisations and management, psychology added another layer to my analysis and unpacking of how organisations operate. I still like and am fascinated by the group dynamic and a bigger picture but I now like to get closer and see how individuals shape roles which might have certain typologies, like leadership for example, and give them their own, individual flavour. The integration between roles and individuals is what fascinates me at the moment. A lot has been said about personalities and how they shape organisational practices, but what I am interested in is the link and interplay between identity and organisational roles and processes. There is something powerful and inspiring in the notion that every individual actively shapes and enacts the world around them. And what PCP gave me is the tools to unpack and understand that process.[134]

2. Make it grow

Poetics
Everything is poetry

According to Aristotle[135], poetics is mimetic, it uses words, rhythms and sounds to represent characters and settings and to evoke feelings in the mind and heart of the reader. The most noble poetic form is, in Aristotle's view, tragedy, with its capacity for catharsis and liberation through the immersion in difficult feelings such as compassion and awe. The poetics of Aristotle is more widely defined than what we nowadays term poetry, and is concerned about different genres of drama and literature. Lyric poetry is but one of them.

In Umberto Eco's[136] categories lyric poetry has one specific, very powerful quality – it is an open work, that is, a text with a multiplicity of meanings and an active, participant audience. It is its openness itself that ultimately defines it: the making of the text takes place within the reading at least as importantly as it does within the writing. It is the reading that brings the open work alive. Poetry is, then, a co-created work of art, and in its initial textual form, an invitation to co-creation. Sappho's genius lies not just in the words she produced but in the fact that her invitation has been and still is accepted by so many readers, from very different places and times, who share little, if anything at all, in terms of cultural capital and social institutions. It does not mean that the reader is entitled to any reading that pleases him or her. I agree with Umberto Eco[137] that any overinterpretation of a text, or reading it with disrespect for the authorial invitation, is not an appropriate use of it. A text can be read critically or immersively, but the reading should remain within the leading idea of the text. In the case of a poetic text, it may very well be that the author from the beginning invites disruptive or drastically aberrant readings. However, that is then part of the text's intent, not a freedom arbitrarily taken with it. In other words, a poetic work is a relationship waiting to happen. It should not be abused; exploitation and maltreatment are not mutual relationships.

The poetic communication is transgressive. According to Michel de Certeau[138] it disconnects the signified from the signifier, going beyond the superficial and down into the hidden domains, the silent and unknown. The poetic has a voice even if it is just a written text, it has a melody and a sound and thus a sensuality that most linear texts do not have. It resounds not just within but against a background. Christopher Caudwell[139] points out that the poetic is based on contradiction between the subject and the context, one which gives birth to rhythm. Words are part of the rhythm, invoking sensations and feelings as if directly, without the mediation of persuasion and rational discourse, just like music. Just like music, it is concentrated affect, opening space for an interaction beyond rational and intellectual communication. Poetry literally moves us: it transmits feelings but also creates a movement in the physical sense of what is very much immaterial: feelings, experiences, impressions, even the mystical.

Poetry often brings hope and inspiration, it has perhaps always been one of their most vital sources. Sappho's poetry was, probably for herself as well as for her readers, a source of hope that love will be reciprocated, that Aphrodite will look kindly upon us. John Burnside's often troubling poetry, reading like something jumping directly out of a dream and touching much more than just the intellect or even the feelings – perhaps the raw naked bones in our bodies, also, in a way not entirely obvious, brings hope of something. Maybe it is vision, and maybe redemption. The dream is suspended where no investigative eye can reach and the poems echo its pulse that at the same time bears witness to our fragility and humanity, but also brings back a tone of something indestructible and ancient, that we also are,

2. Make it grow

at the core, and one day will return to. The poems lead the way and radiate a premonition of its timeless language.

One of my favourite poets, Rumi, speaks directly of that timelessness. In one of his poems, he renounces the dark state of mind springing from hopelessness.

If you are seeking, seek us with joy
For we live in the kingdom of joy.
Do not give your heart to anything else
But to the love of those who are clear joy,
Do not stray into the neighbourhood of despair.
For there are hopes: they are real, they exist —
Do not go in the direction of darkness —
I tell you: suns exist[140.]

A good friend of mine, who is a Benedictine monk in northern Scotland, has told me about one of the main sins, as seen by the mystics – a state of dark futility, which is known as acedia. The cited poem by Rumi, also a mystic, promises to lead the seeker away from it, indeed it does more than that for anyone who reads these words aloud.

Poetic organizing

Henderson's Relish is a popular condiment, produced in Sheffield since the late nineteenth century by a family-owned business. Although it has been changing ownership over the 100 years of its existence, it always remained faithfully local and personally controlled. The brand is much loved by the people of South Yorkshire, considered a must at every lunch and dinner table. It has a following among chefs, even cookbooks dedicated to its use, and a number of local artists, professionals and amateurs use it as a motif in cartoons, still lives and depictions of Sheffield streets. It has featured in a popular BBC entertainment series, created by a Sheffield-born comedian. It also appears on T-shirts, postcards and posters, some of them intended as promotional material and produced by Hendersons Ltd, but some created independently. People actually wear these T-shirts and many take great pride in the local associations of the brand. Sheffield is also famous for its thriving graffiti scene, with artists such as Kid Acne, Phlegm and Rocket01 among famous street artists with roots in the city. There are many spots in the city centre which serve as exhibition points, where paintings tend to appear spontaneously. In one of these spots, in November 2017, a sticker art popped up, representing a long-necked model, associated with a well-known fragrance brand, now, with a bottle of Henderson's instead of perfume, in her hand. The text says: "Relish the flavor" and displays a white Yorkshire rose. This image is most definitely created in the genre of an advertisement, using not only the tropes but also the actual picture of an existing ad. It is not an example of the more widely spread ad-busting variety of graffiti, as it does not seek to mock, it is not ironic or critical. It genuinely praises the brand and places it within two contexts: that of beauty and the good life, and the local context of South Yorkshire. However, it is a defiant image: it uses copyrighted corporate material for its own purposes, and it makes a rebellious point – the condiment is a good replacement for the expensive corporate brand for helping people to enjoy a good life. The beautiful model seems perfectly at peace with the bottle of Hendo's; her beatific smile is, at last, understandable – she simply relishes the condiment. Such a show of love and dedication cannot be planned, ordered, managed into being, it loses its momentum as soon as it is subjected to measure, ranking or inspection. In fact, doing any of these things dramatically decreases the probability of the unprompted love not just finding an expression but blossoming up at all. This spontaneous marketing is a good example that poetry and management, or the firm, marketing, etc., are not as much apart as one would often assume nowadays. It is just that the type of management that currently dominates is utterly unpoetic.

Organization theorist Heather Höpfl[141] proposes that the Aristotelean distinction of two modes of communication, the rhetorical and the poetic, has a relevance for how social life is organized and managed. Rhetorics is about persuasion, control, ordering, and represents a way of communication that is typical of traditional, hierarchical organizations. Poetics opens the mind, explodes categories, helps to see what is not in plain sight. It makes us aware of the value of ambivalence and ambiguity, rather than seeking to eradicate it as does rhetorical management. Ambivalence invites inspiration, opens the doors of perception to imagination. It does not try to limit and cleanse but welcomes new insights and ideas. This is how real innovation is born: out of humility and openness to something bigger than the individual human mind. At the same time, poetics, as art more generally, provides a tool for the shaping of a collective identity not based on exclusion and xenophobia. A poetic collective identity does not have to eradicate difference, because it invokes a greater good, a greater common denominator. Poetic thinking makes room for a different mode of organizing and managing, based on this kind of collective identity. While rhetorical management is linear, seeks to order, persuade and establish structure, poetic management is about coherence without control, content before form, dedication without suppression.[142] Poetic management can be invoked but not used, it is not a tool, rather, a mindset, inviting imagination and employing higher emotions. It is not about hegemony but about responsibility and rhythm: adapting to the collective flows and acknowledging the existence of a greater whole. This opens up space for true creativity. Rhetorical management all too often harms creative work, even if it boasts of enhancing creative effectivity, because it is fixated on activities damaging to creativity, such as detailed planning, streamlining, eradicating all elements that are not rational in a reductionist, linear fashion – in Heather Höpfl's words, an obsessive filling in of empty spaces[143]. Poetic managers do not accept that as a sound state of mind, they long for something different, which is, alas, all too often absent from their textbooks and professional magazines.

For many people the role of poetry is that of opening up paths which are absent from the everyday world. It has always been, and still is, a reservoir of hope. Joanna Średnicka[144] has studied ethnographically a large Polish industrial corporation, with a long and variable history. There were times, remembered by the employees as the golden era, when the economy of the company was improving, new ideas flowing in, and they were an independent organization, with the power to shape their own future. These days are now sadly gone and people recall them with sorrow. But also with hope, which they express by referring, more or less explicitly, to the work of the great Polish romantic poet Adam Mickiewicz. He wrote poetry of resistance and hope in a time when Poland was divided up between its three powerful neighbours. His epic poem *Pan Tadeusz* published in the first half of the nineteenth century brings back visions of a time more innocent and happier, when hope was much more obvious. By recreating the aura of this time, he put a powerful dream in the minds and hands of the readers. Joanna was surprised, and then enthralled, to find that today's rational and otherwise quite rhetorically predisposed managers looked to Mickiewicz's poetry in the same way as the oppressed Poles of the nineteenth century – to find a strong and direct link to a state of mind beyond simple consent or compliance. She explains to me in a conversation we have about her thesis:

> Yes. Even though the last time they've read Mickiewicz was probably in school; or with their kids, more recently. But this remains in the DNA. Today I was visiting my mum and I ate doughnuts she's made. I can't cook but, entirely naturally, I asked, how do you make such doughnuts? They taste just like granny's. It's because it's granny's recipe. When mum started to list things she's been doing, she didn't have to continue. The images from my childhood returned: gran's warm kitchen, yeast, sour cream. Doughnuts growing up on the pastry board. It's in the DNA. Like images from *Pan Tadeusz.* Quick to wake up and spring to life again.

Heather Höpfl[145] speaks of what it is important to wake up *towards.* A failing system, a devastated natural world, people suffering from appalling management practices. Poetic organizing and managing carries the promise of changing all this, and of real sustainability. Rhetorical management is wasteful, as it is a reductive strategy, it aims at doing away with everything that cannot be contained in strict limits of embraced standards. It rejects and renounces all that falls beyond its streamlined idea of productive output, avoiding everything that is ambiguous and relentlessly reducing complexity. Organizations managed this way cannot adapt to a complex environment, which today is the norm. Instead of using all of its resources in an adaptable manner, they do away with everything that surpasses rigid benchmarks, including professional judgement, engagement, commitment and perspectives. Poetics also has the potential of bringing attention to marginalized and silenced standpoints. Such voices are needed for a more inclusive participation, and they often bring new ideas, important for change and regeneration of the entire system. Getting rid of poetics means forsaking self-regeneration and renewal in a situation of crisis.

Furthermore, if we conceive of strategy as a kind of common narrative thrust for the organization, then rhetorics stand for the unidirectional dynamics, movement towards what is well known or at least can be anticipated. If no such movement is possible, as it is today, in a world that has lost its internal compass, what we are left with is a chaotic state, with no working social institutions, a stark fragmentation and privatization of intent. In times like these, only poetics are able to offer a viable strategy at all. In Heather Höpfl's words:

In poetics the meaning is always ambivalent and resonates with the flux of experience[146].

Instead of just opening up the doors for the unexpected, inviting pure chaos and entropy, poetic management is selective in its invitations. It is sensitive to flows and rhythms which are not always able to even put into words. It relies on a connection for humans through sadness, joy, compassion, rebellion, etc. It is a unity of principle rather than of slogan, aim or presentation of self. Poetry is, in the words of Scottish poet John Burnside, an ecology, a science of belonging[147]. Art is not a political pursuit, but it is nonetheless a political act, as it presents us with shared visions of worlds other than the linear and superficial and presents us with a common idea, a bond with all living things in ways out of grasp for rhetorical discourse. Mystery should not, cannot, be eliminated and it is poetry's role to remind us of it.

> The more we know, the more the mystery deepens...teaches us part of the duty of dwelling, it teaches us a necessary awe.[148]

By giving us a sense of belonging connected with the feeling of belonging, it inspires rebellion, resistance, a recognition of being human as an ecological act. Thus poetry helps us to change the world, even if in a tiny way.

It sounds like something extraordinarily complicated but it need not be. It is a matter of attention and discipline in the approach rather than pre-emptive design. For example, in the mid-noughties, a Swedish public sector organization was drawn into the whirlpool of new public management, cuts, bureaucratization, insistence of competition and of treating the public as customers. The new manager was a true crusader of NPM methods and values and changes were carried out swiftly and unhesitantly, taking the employees by surprise. They were used to a very different style of management, consultations about all matters, big, small and trivial. The new manager consulted them on some of his policies, got a strong no, then ignored it completely, not even making the results public in one case, in others, re-packaging the no as if to pass it off as a yes. People were confused, perhaps even shocked. There were some attempts at protest but they were soon silenced by disciplining actions. The new boss soon got a following of dedicated young supporters, who saw him and his actions as an excellent opportunity to fast track their own careers. He was feared, hated even, but no one contradicted him. People felt powerless and believed that this was inevitable: what the spirit of the times was bringing. He himself did much to further this attitude. Many of the meetings were in fact ideological gatherings, opportunities to school the employees in the use of the new terms and ideas, make them familiar with and reconciled with them, a force majeure, an irresistible dynamic, better to be observed than resisted. The new boss not only broke the people's spines but also their morale. Never before had it been so difficult to manage this organization, never before had people been so reluctant, devoid of trust and joy. And so, one day, as it often is with managers of this kind, the new boss got promoted and disappeared into the higher echelons of the public sector. The organization remained without a manager. Nobody was willing to volunteer, it was in really bad shape, people were dispirited, there were rumours of bullying and numerous wrong doings, including unethical if not downright illegal handling of public funds. Nobody wanted to take responsibility for the mess. Finally, the higher-up boss made up his mind, something needed to be done and fast. So he invited Björn, an older man about to retire, for a chat at his office.

"Björn", he said, "I know this does not come as a happy surprise for you, but we really need you to do this for us. Your whole career you have been dedicated to this unit. Please take over. I don't take no for an answer."

Indeed, it wasn't a nice surprise. And indeed, he did not refuse. Björn was a kind, warm-hearted man, a responsible man. Faced with the impossible task, he did what he had to do – he took over the abandoned office and he took the people to his heart. The first thing that happened, almost overnight, as if spring had suddenly come, was that the bragging ceased. What had seemed to be a solid and incessant stream of self-promotion, on all media and occasions, just stopped. Instead, people went to Björn to tell him about their successes, their fears, their hopes, and he listened to them all. He talked with everyone: the stars, the underdogs, the bullied, the bullies, the supporters of the ex-boss. He listened and he knew what to do from their stories, ideas and complaints.

He made sure the bullying ceased, using the institutional means at his disposal. And he gave people a sense of stability, as well as paths to a career that attracted some of the bullies and made them focus their energy. Others, the ones with sociopathic tendencies, just left. One, the worst offender, was submitted to a formal procedure and made to leave. Björn held many meetings but not of the standard business-talk kind. They were dedicated to the discussion of important matters, most of all, the aims of the unit. The spirit of public service was brought back into the department. A comedy club was soon organized and informal comedy evenings brought together all the employees. They laughed at everything but most of all, they laughed at power. Björn laughed the most at jokes aimed at himself, especially a kind-hearted yet satirical little song about "mother hen". It was he who was the mother hen of the department, taking care of all, guiding it wherever the spirit of public service took them. And so it was until he retired, even in these difficult times of public sector cuts and the dissolution of structures. Then things went downhill again, but he was remembered since by all as proof that things can be done differently, always.

Poetic organizing is based not just on the visible, such as strategies and structures, but also on what cannot be seen: silence, empty spaces. Heather Höpfl[149] speaks of silence as being the pathway to a space profoundly and inherently human, a mode of being rather than a characteristic, a slogan, something that can be used as typical "business talk"[150] so it is not easily translatable to mainstream management wisdom. Reflecting upon the role of emptiness in organizing[151], I propose that organizations can be seen as an empty stage, the way that Peter Brook saw it:

In everyday life, "if" is a fiction, in the theatre "if" is an experiment. In everyday life, "if" is an evasion, in the theatre "if" is the truth. When we are persuaded to believe in this truth, then the theatre and life are one. This is a high aim. It sounds like hard work. To play needs much work. But when we experience the work as play, then it is not work anymore. A play is play[152].

It opens the door to the staging of organizing seen as ongoing process, involving both known scenarios and improvisations. It is:

> unclassified and unclaimed, the margin where change can be initiated. Seen this way, it is not a cleared away space, or a spot wiped clean of all things, rather a perception absent of expectations, open to an ambivalent interpretation of reality[153].

Rather than being "nothing" it is an invitation and opening, not through clearing away, rationalizing, cuts or austerity but by making room through liminality. Liminality is the state betwixt and between more stable states and realities[154]. It has no finite qualities, its boundaries are blurred, the constraints of normality, common sense and cultural definitions are temporarily lifted. This is a condition common in the process of creation of culture through ritual, especially in the middle phase during rites of passage, or rituals marking the transition between social roles, for example from single to married, from student to absolvent[155]. Such moments are very intense culturally, with a particular openness to experimentation and a great potential to generate a sense of community. A special bond is developed by people going through this stage together, known as *communitas,* inclusive, based on bonds of humanity, disregarding difference of rank, position and formal structure. Organizing by empty space is, first of all, about leaving deliberately unmanaged physical spaces, fragments of roles, and slots of time. There awaits a potentiality: liminality to happen, an indefinite moment which may, or may not, give birth to experiments, new interpretations and uses. It may also become reclaimed by underdogs, underlings, or simply omitted from formal management and recreated by people as a cultural sanctuary or symbolic retreat.

English organization theorist Heather Höpfl[156] regarded liminality as the birthplace of poetics as well as organizing. Yet she saw that contemporary management is utterly inept at handling it.

> In the relentless pursuit of future states, organizations as purposive entities seek to construct for themselves the empty emblems of the object of the quest. In part, this is because the purposiveness is without end and, therefore, the notion of any real completion is antithetical to the idea of trajectory. Strategy gives birth to more strategy, rhetoric to more rhetoric and text to more text and so on. The sublime is never attained. The individual in the organization is always constituted in unworthiness, always deficient in relation to the constructed sublime.[157]

Only the sublime can help to attain the sublime. The path towards redemption and enlightenment is, by itself, inspiring and miraculous. The journey is its own end, and yet, if undertaken, it does lead to something beyond and outside of itself. Poetry and poetic organizing are about crossing the boundaries of what is known and tamed, it is sublime and dangerous, but it has the power to open new horizons and, doing that, it brings hope in its form as dream. Dreams can be dreamed while asleep but they can also awaken us to the simple and powerful truth about the human condition: we are not defined. There is always something that evades definition in us. That "something" is much greater than the narrow and linear contents of the taken for granted. It comes up in grand visions (or the lack of them), in aspirations and values. But most often, it surfaces in the mundane and everyday real.

In a small, privately-owned consulting firm in the south of England, the partners liked working together and were happy about the freedom and the responsibility in doing their job that the partnership gave them, but they often felt out of place in their office. They invested in a fashionable designer. It was nice, but there was still a grating feeling, vague and indefinite. They did away with the transparent walls, replacing them with white partition walls, and decorated them with art by their favourite graffiti artists. That helped a lot. But it was still not it.

At one meeting, Anna, one of the partners said: "There is something wrong with the space. It feels...sticky somehow."

"Sticky!, haha!" another partner, Brian, laughed, "Should be dusted, then?"

They all laughed because the proposition seemed so absurd, the office was being regularly cleaned, there was no dust anywhere in sight and everything smelled of cleaning substances and deodorant. But, somehow, this idea made them all think. Finally, Stephen spoke up:

"It sure is being dusted. But, you know, just dusted, not *cared for*."

They all looked up, in a sudden revelation.

"Let's hire a permanent cleaner!" Anna exclaimed.

"Or two!" Brian suggested.

"That's a brilliant idea!" Rob declared, "but why call them cleaners? There is no problem with cleanliness. We have a problem with space! Let's call them space carers."

And so they did. They terminated the contract with the cleaning company and hired two full- time employees to take care of the space in the office, Bella and Flo. In the beginning, Bella and Flo were just cleaning the offices; however, they were not just thorough but also started to feel responsible. Bella, the younger one, demanded eco-friendly cleaning materials. The partners were amazed no one had thought about it before. Of course they wanted the cleaning to be eco-friendly! They felt good about it, and the smell improved, too. Then Bella and Flo started to be increasingly self-confident, slightly bossy, Brian complained to Anna. They were a bit uncomfortable with it in the beginning but got used to it very fast. It was as it should be – Bella and Flo were taking care of the space, not just cleaning. They ordered the people occupying the space around, a little bit, told them off, when they did not recycle a whole pile of old papers properly, or left a smelly, rotting carrot in the fridge. They were the hosts here. The partners felt a strong presence in their office space: "I feel at home here now," as Anna put it.

When spring came, the partners noticed tiny plants coming up by the building's entrance. Bella and Flo had claimed the bit of land in front of the house and were planting flowers and vegetables, turning it into a little street garden. They were, after all, not cleaners, they were taking care of the space.

Art
What is art?

What is art? This is a question that many have asked, philosophers and laymen, but it keeps on popping up in discourses high and low, with no hope of a resolution in sight. Which is perhaps a good sign indeed as, whatever art is, it is definitely not what can be easily framed and defined. If it has a recurring role in human history, it is that of awakening questions and disturbing straightforward orders. The theorist of art John Ruskin[158] upheld that art was a kind of communication, using different media to convey a profound truth about humanity and nature that is to be found beyond them both, at a deeper and invisible level. He saw painting as a language and a vehicle for thought, with no particular meaning in itself. Its greatness lies in its ability to express and invoke ideas and move the higher faculties of the human mind. This is a view that has kept some of its allure but is rarely considered to be in touch with the work of the modern artist and able to convey its value and role in society. More contemporarily, the art critic and poet John Berger[159], saw art as most of all something unique that carries original meaning. There is no "correct" way to create art, or to take it in, read it and look at it. The meaning emerges in the relationship between the artist and the viewer and is neither static nor depersonalized. Yes, the meaning that art carries may be deeper than the mundane and superficial layers of culture, but it is not a fixed essence but, rather, something the artist saw. It is deeply personal but also, at heart, something profoundly true. This is also how the viewer may see it if the work of art captures her or him.

We only see what we look at. To look is an act of choice[160].

Art is, thus, a representation of how we, actively, see things.

John Berger was an artist, art critic and storyteller with an ability to see and understand the world of art in a way with deep sociological implications. He was kind, compassionate and engaged. He was also, for many readers, a bringer of hope, an author who did not fail to see and understand the gravity of our times' problems, and certainly did not withhold from speaking out, but who always understood that there is an alternative, that we can find a way out of the seemingly impossible global impasse. He spoke to us about it through art. He was building bridges between politics, society, different places and times from art and explained how he was able to do it and how we, his readers and listeners, can find a way of doing that for ourselves. Such is the ground-breaking nature of his BBC programme and then book *Ways of seeing*[161], where he shows how art is not only an aesthetic experience but very much a political and social one, with resonances in everyday life and implications for how we can think of the future. Art, to him, is a way of bringing agency to the viewers, messages of emancipation and experience across different contexts. But it is also a way of opening doors and windows between worlds, looking into the world of the artist, yet without transplanting the meaning. The onlooker keeps and creates her or his own meaning, in her or his time and space The artwork is the impossible interface between them, what unites realities and persons who may not have anything else in common. The artwork can even help the onlooker to express their own world. Berger also believed that art can help us to change the world, by reaching beyond the obvious and connecting the unconnectable.

The favourite painter of John Berger was Caravaggio[162], also among my absolute favourites. Berger explains that Caravaggio's work brings to us the lives of the dispossessed, people who are used to sharing space, at home in shadows which give shelter as well as walls. The people in his paintings are apostles, saints, Jesus himself, but they are all depicted as poor people, living like the poor still do, close to each other, with intense gestures, not unlike theatre where everyone is playing out a presence among others and legends.

Berger was 90 when he died but in all the later films and pictures of him he was keeping his youth, at the same time as he was getting old. He was becoming himself much like the artworks he so admired: a beautiful elder, a thrust of energy, an embodiment of ambiguity, the teller of hope. In that he stays with us, even if no longer here, just like a work of art. This is profoundly human, in his own words:

> We live – if one follows the biblical sequence of events – after the Fall. In any case, we live in a world of suffering in which evil is rampant, a world whose events do not confirm our Being, a world that has to be resisted. It is in this situation that the aesthetic moment offers hope[163.]

And he left us a gift, smuggled in between worlds, to be used as much as we wish, and to be forwarded further, as he put it:

"hope is a contraband passed from hand to hand and story to story"[164].

Organizing by Art

She leads me down the stairs with a light, almost dancing step. I follow, much less gracefully, already in awe of the vast interiors of the theatre building. She is at home here, seems to be greeting every corner, and they are many in this complicated, labyrinthine building. The corridors are long and ending in sudden turns in a direction that is completely counterintuitive. The light is strange, ominous in places, bright and schoolroom-like in others. Ewa is like a small white rabbit, in a dress that seems to be changing colour depending on the light, and I almost have to run to keep up with her. She shows me service passages, dusty storage rooms (we have to use our flashlights on our mobile phones here) and fantastic theatrical props with the same admiration and respect. She shakes her arm, almost in a ballet dancer's studied motion, at a chandelier.

"Look, look, it is almost flat, you see?" she says and I discover, walking around it, that it is, indeed, flat. From far it looks so irresistibly real and from up close you can see it is fake, but not the shopping centre kind of fake. Different.

"Take a look at the room now," she says. I do and I see what she means – from where I am standing now, everything looks like from the other side of the mirror in Lewis Carroll's book. This is no fake. This is magic.

Then she jumps up again and starts moving very fast. I follow, still dazed with the sensation of having been part of something very unusual, very much beyond the rational world. There are flowing shadows on the walls, yes, I see that the walls are dilapidated and the floors in need of a good renovation. I remember such interior decorating material from my student years and they are, well, a bit distant in time. Then she flashes me a smile, as elusive as her step. She stands still now. I look around. I know where I am – and I know nothing about it. We smile at each other. We are standing in the middle of the great stage of the theatre. From where I stand, I can see the beautifully decorated auditorium where I used to sit so many times, since I was little, watching the people who were standing and moving around right where we are now. It looks much smaller from this vantage point, and much less obvious, more like an afterthought, a glorious appendage, no longer as *the* theatre. So, we are standing on the stage. It is a place where people work. A workplace.

The constant and powerful presence of decorations, props and close relationships with art is what characterizes what Pierre Guillet de Monthoux[165] terms the artfirm. It is usually an organization dedicated to artistic endeavours, such as theatres, art galleries, concert halls, but any organization can strive to become an artfirm. Organizing has an artistic aspect and management can become an artform. Guillet de Monthoux, referring to Immanuel Kant, argues that aesthetics occupies the space between scientific truth and the moral realm. It has the great advantage to be able to be made visible and so to perform the role of a perceptible moral compass for employees and managers, who look for inspiration to solve the dilemma: how to be innovative yet moral, organized yet creative. Filling the space with aesthetic sensations, not necessarily art in the strict sense, can be a way to provide such a compass. Instead of worship, knowledge or ideology, just being there, being present in a space suffused with a sense of the artistic, can serve as an inspiration and reservoir of ideas on how to find a balance between the seeming unconnectables.

Art is a way of seeing and narrating the world around us. It can communicate aspects of it that no rational discourse is able to convey: the emotional, irrational, intuitive and aesthetic. According to Pierre Guillet de Monthoux[166] all human endeavours have an aesthetic dimension, and organizing is no exception to the rule. It just so happens that it is usually portrayed one-sidedly, with an almost complete oversight of everything beyond the rational surface. Enterprises devoid of aesthetics are not just incomplete, but inhuman and thus incomprehensible. We are not able to grasp management without understanding art, Guillet de Monthoux persuades, economic development without an aesthetic perspective makes no sense. This was clear to the founders of economics, including Adam Smith who was very much aware of the complexity and art of economic actions. Good managers know it too, even if they are not educated to deal with it or even allowed to express it in many circumstances. Aesthetics has a moral aspect that best belongs together with a sense of beauty, otherwise it risks turning into an empty and coercive normative approach, resulting in an orientation towards rules and regulations supposedly safeguarding moral behaviour. Bureaucracy does not replace or support morality, often the opposite is the case. The actors invoke "just following the rules" to suppress their conscience and moral compass. A manager should be aware of this and managerial talent is very much connected to the ability to move others and bring them beyond what is mundane and common and towards what is merely possible. Indeed, Pierre Guillet de Monthoux suggests that management is "a journey in aesthetic space[167]". Seen this way, it is to a large extent aesthetic, creative action. Managers, not supported or educated in this respect, turn to one of two common strategies: of exclusion or inclusion. The first means excluding art from one's everyday managerial experience. The latter consists of turning art into yet one more resource, that can be bought and sold, which has a price tag and can be subjected to similar techniques as design management or logistics. Both strategies turn art into a mysterious black box that remains unknown and unknowable, can be expelled from the essence of managerial occupations, either as an object of worship or something devoid of relevance. Neither of these approaches

2. Make it grow

helps us to understand or develop a relationship with art that can enhance and enrich management. It should instead be recognized that management without art is deficient and even meaningless. Approaching managerial duties from an aesthetic perspective not only helps to avoid the trap of boredom and lack of imagination, but it also helps to accept and even appreciate that humans are much more than machines, costs or resources. Art has the unique capacity to at the same time inspire creativity and instil modesty.

It also has another interesting and very valuable feature that comes in handy in contemporary management of organizations. As Ceri Watkins, Ian King and Stephen Linstead[168] argue, it makes it possible to deal with a complex reality without reducing the complexity. It offers the possibility of manageability without simplification. And so it may serve as an alternative to the reductionist logic of the dominant management models, filling in the gap between world perception and human experience in all kinds of organizations[169]. Furthermore, it inspires creativity. I agree with Stefan Svallfors[170] that no management policy or strategy, no matter how brilliant, is able to bring about innovation and creativity – it is, just like happiness, a side product of something else. This "something else" can be artistic interventions in organizations. Stefan Meisek and Daved Barry[171] explain that such interventions help the social actors to see their everyday reality from a different point of view, thus bringing about a range of effects, from entertainment to catharsis. All these can result in creativity and innovation, but do not have to. It is a kind of a carnival, a temporary lifting of rules, testing out things that are not usual within given limits.

Of course, there is no guarantee that an art lover will be a good human being, or that he or she will persevere on the path of modest creativity. Peter Pelzer[172] points out that, in the capitalist world, art is the weaker partner of business. It is business that rules the world and has the ability to buy other areas of life, including art. Thus art can help to banalize business, become kitsch, fallen and corrupt, degraded to the role of claqueur.

Stefan Meisek and Daved Barry[173] present an experiment in inviting art into organizational settings on a temporary, carnivalesque basis. A Danish government organization had, in response to a problem with a persisting deficit in communication between two departments, launched an organizational studio, run by representatives from both departments and based on the ideas of one of the authors. It was called Det Nye Rum, The New Room, because they "liked the physical connotation[174]". It was limited in time and space and would allow people to talk differently, about different things, even eat different things and act differently than usual for the duration. In the words of one of the participants:

> We didn't really know what it is actually but it has something to do with solving wicked problems and creative methods for doing it...not reducing complexity but actually taking in complexity.[175]

The project team introduced the artistic intervention themselves, without a visiting artist. But they could use the advice of a researcher who would at times challenge them and provoke them to see things from another perspective. This could be at times frustrating but proved to be quite effective. People who, until now, did not talk to each other due to a lack of a common language, now had intensive contact with each other for the duration of the event. At a certain point the advisor was no longer needed and the studio was working well all by itself. It was a "bubble, a universe separate from the rest of the organization[176]", disconnecting the participants from the habitual work experience and inviting artistic inquiry. They dedicated their energy towards talking about important issues from all perspectives they could think of, without being stopped or criticized, without restrictive generalization or premature conclusions. Soon they started to develop connections between each other and were coming up with new ideas and solutions to "unsolvable" problems in the form of models. They used low cost artistic materials for their expressions, such as Styrofoam and ribbons, creating them as both useful and beautiful objects. The intervention was successful in creating new openings where they were thought of as impossible before, not just for the duration of the project. It "took on a life of its own"[177]. A year after the intervention a new organizational solution appeared that would be greeted as a most welcome innovation. They had been trying to achieve this so many times before but had not been successful until they experimented with the artistic intervention. This is an example of art actually helping to solve an important organizational problem. It does not always go that far. Sometimes it does not bring any concrete practical solutions, yet, still, it makes all the difference because of its presence in the organization. It brings and embodies hope that another world is possible, as in the second example.

Stockholm School of Economics Art Initiative[178] describe themselves as a team who:

> explores and develops transboundary knowledge exchange, production and transfer through art and the humanities. We generate art exhibitions and symposiums directed towards researchers, students and the public.[179]

They explain their mission as provoking, questioning and inspiring through the tools of art and the humanities and thus developing sociological and economic imagination, enhancing the capacity to think beyond the linear rationality that so often limits and even drags down economists around the world. Stockholm School of Economics has different aspirations and the Art Initiative is thought of as a way of supporting thinking in terms of complexity rather than reductionism, by bringing together people and institutions from science and the arts.

> SSE Art Initiative aims at making students aware and attracted by art as an aesthetic source of knowledge. Sometimes beautiful, but frequently also irritating and strange, the confrontation with art suddenly flings open new widows to unmapped realities[180].

The events organized by the initiative range from seminars and art talks, via exhibitions, acquisition of artwork, to concerts, to parties, such as the Dada Party organized close to Christmas in one of the school's social spaces. There was music, spontaneous poetry, live performances, film and, of course, glögg – the famous Swedish version of mulled wine. What was particularly heartening to me was the diversity of the people attending and organizing: they could not be limited to an age group, nationality or occupation. There were students, artists, academics, there were a few children, and the atmosphere was that of a real carnival, to which all seemed to be equally dedicated.

Music
Music for the lively mind
Poetry and music used to be closely connected. The poems of Sappho, Sumerian hymns, David's psalms, verses of the Odyssey – all used to be sung.

> Music, for one thing. For the Greeks, the "lyric" in "lyric poetry" was literal: the verses were composed to be sung to the accompaniment of a lyre[181],

explains David Mendelsohn in an article in *The New Yorker*. Poems used to have a rhythmic scheme, which the poets themselves sometimes invented, as is the case with the sapphic stanza.

When poetry and music went their partly separate ways (some poetry is still meant to be sung, such as the songs of Leonard Cohen), music came to stand for the pure spirit. "Music expresses that which cannot be put into words and that which cannot remain silent," wrote Victor Hugo,[182] "It is to poetry what reverie is to thought, what the fluid is to the liquid, what the ocean of clouds is to the ocean of waves.[183]" In an essay published in the late eighteenth century dedicated to musical criticism, Charles Avison[184] defines music by melody, harmony and modulation, cadences and passages, which he explains as methods of producing and linking sounds, not unlike speaking or writing. However, to him music is also like painting. "They are both founded in geometry,"[185] he proclaims, founded on proportions and waves and vibrations, and they both rely on expression, which is the work of invention shaped out of design and composition. They seek for harmony and create their own distances and their own subject.

Music is unique in its capacity to speak almost the same language as human emotions. In a text on different artists' ideas about what music is, Terri Paglush[186] cites Leonard Cohen, who declared that "music is the emotional life of most people". For John Coltrane, his:

> music is the spiritual expression of what I am – my faith, my knowledge, my being...When you begin to see the possibilities of music, your desire to do something really good for people, to help humanity free itself from its hangups ...I want to speak to their souls.[187]

Similarly, Ray Charles considers music part of himself, while Ludwig von Beethoven regarded it a "higher revelation than all wisdom and philosophy"[188]. It is not too strange, then, to look to music with the aim of finding ideas of hope. Or, to see whether music and organizing together create spaces for hope.

Music and organizing

"It's not my revolution if I can't dance to it," said Emma Goldman, anarcho-socialist and feminist born in Lithuania at the end of the nineteenth century. Actually, she did not say the exact words, it is a paraphrase of a longer utterance. But I imagine she would not have anything against being cited as author of this famous aphorism. Emma's revolution was an idea of lightness and energy, and so is mine, even if I do not agree with all of her convictions. Unlike her, I believe in structures and social institutions. And, also unlike her, I am not a person who enjoys dancing. I never have. I have always been the one who spends parties discussing the end of capitalism and Led Zeppelin's last album in the kitchen. I do not have a sense of rhythm, nor of balance, so dancing is not a favourite pastime of mine, nor do I know of anyone who would dream of dancing the night away with me. However, a few times in my life my feet would start to dance all by themselves. First time it happened, it was the music of the summer of love. Not the popular tunes that made everyone else jump, but stuff that killed the dancing party, when someone decided to play Pink Floyd's *Echoes* or Led Zeppelin's *Stairway to Heaven*. I would dance all alone to *Set the Controls to the Hearts of the Sun*, I could not resist Jim Morrison's melorecitations. The same thing happened when I was listening to these songs by myself. I would jump up and dance.

The second time it happened more recently, when I heard Captain SKA's *Liar, Liar,* just before the UK snap election of 2017. I would jump up and dance, even in the middle of writing, or when I was really tired and literally falling asleep; I could not help myself, the music made me dance the moment I heard it. Before the election results which so shocked the UK media and the ruling party, the unexpectedly good result of the "unelectable" Jeremy Corbyn, my feet knew this moment had the right energy. The song itself made it to number four on the UK singles chart, even though it was absent from the major radio stations, including the BBC. Its lively rhythm and melodic mockery of a politics of lies and contempt promised that something fresher was on its way. This simple song of resistance to alienation, to unnecessary suffering and to the glorification of disdain communicated an energy that electrified my feet into dancing.

A third moment when my feet feel like dancing is when I visit a co-operative organization in central Warsaw, which is one of the alternative economic organizations I have been studying for the last 5 years. They are a consumers' co-operative serving as intermediaries in the trade of fresh ecological food. They currently operate two very successful shops in Warsaw and consist of more than 250 members, who regularly support the co-operative with their work, time and engagement. They have a democratic, decentralized structure and their organizing principles consist of a set of radical values, taken very seriously by the participants, such as the dedication to the production and consumption of healthy ecological food, and a belief in a more just society and economy that will replace capitalism. They consider work to be a human right and a value and actively support workers' rights. During my study, I have worked with the co-op members several times, helping out with the physical jobs in the shops. Sometimes I visit them as a customer, to buy fresh agricultural produce. Quite often, my feet want to dance. It may be so because of the music that is usually played here: reggae, ska, rock. But there is something else beyond that – a sense of dynamic harmony, of people and things corresponding with each other, a synchronized sense of belonging.

What do these three experiences share in common, which makes me feel like dancing? Maybe it is a sense of things falling into place around me, involving me, not so much in the material, as in the spiritual sense. The music of the 1960s was very much inspired by the Romantics: not only did The Doors take their name after William Blake's poetry, but much of the poetics of the era was about the opening of the doors of perception. Captain SKA's song was a factor in contributing to the spreading of the Momentum movement in the UK, working in favour of Jeremy Corbyn's Labour. Jeremy Corbyn who, famously, cited Percy Bysshe Shelley at the Glastonbury Festival in June 2017. Finally, the co-operative is an embodied, organic act of bold imagination in its inclusive, radical creation of new structural forms, its everyday poetics. These movements and organizations are all profoundly revolutionary, but neither violent nor calculated. They have a lightness which has nothing to do with distance or irony. Music is a way of registering the feeling of the dynamics of organizing.

I am of course not the only organization theorist to have discovered this. Two researchers from Sweden, Tommy Jensen and Johan Sandström, have been co-operating for several years in a study focused on power and labour relations in the mining industry. They have been particularly interested in the non-obvious relationship between power structures and the embodied, material aspect of mining. At a certain point, they felt it would be good to illustrate one of the presentations (we showed a video clip, filmed in Kiruna, showing how they tear down a part of the town because of the mining activities, talked about method, at an "after method" workshop held in Västerås) they were holding about their research with music. They tried open access music but were disappointed. Then Tommy Jensen, who is himself a musician, playing several musical instruments and especially the guitar, singing and composing music, came up with the obvious idea – to create the music themselves, as part of the project, instead of just "writing it up"[189]. They run a blog dedicated to the project, which they regularly update with short descriptions of findings as well as photographs and songs[190]. The aim of the study is about trying to see patterns where linear logic does not reach:

the starting point for this project is that the rocks might remain the same over the years, but that the organizing of them in time and space does not. Accommodating organizing rocks in the new world of work, the project highlights power relations in labour processes, but in terms of hybridized labour processes and hybridized power relations (where there is a readiness for these processes and relations to cross established spatial and temporal organizational and methodological boundaries). The project can therefore be thought of as a mobile study of power relations in labour processes in an apparently immobile industry. Three questions and related purposes are set forth in the project.[191]

They have, until the date of the writing of these words, produced three albums: *Spaceland, Production* and *Gruvan, makten och samhället* (*The mine, power, and society*), all dated 2016. They held several concerts in Poland and in Sweden, at universities, in clubs and in the cultural centre at one of the mining sites where the research is being carried out. Apart from music, they also include visual media in the presentation of their findings, and they have had two exhibitions of their work, with mixed media, photography and music. The music is good and worth listening to for its own sake – I should recommend you, dear Reader, to try! It is melodic, it has a clear and oftentimes quite emphatic rhythm and is very earthy. As ethnographic script, it has a further and unique role – it carries meaning that otherwise would probably not have been possible to express, especially not by traditional written report. Tommy Jensen, asked what he would recommend other ethnographers do in order to better get to know the sounds and rhythms of their field, gave the following advice:

Record the sounds of the field! That I can recommend. I have been down in the mine to record the sounds of the mountains but it did not work out well. So I mimicked the described sounds – the mountain sounds different depending on the level – through distorted guitar, and added spoken vocals based on the account of one of the interviewees telling us that when she got a new work place, further down the ground, the sound of the mountain scares her seriously. However, I did record the sounds of the works. Including sounds does something to you as a researcher, it is as the "field" opens up, becomes more rich, a wider spectra to draw from. Also, crafting short stories – rock lyrics – enables you to write about stuff that rarely makes it, particularly scientific articles, but for sure also books. Further, as in my case, writing lyrics, putting music to them, and then to use the body to play and sing them, makes the empirical field vibrate in your "whole being". A full body experience, somehow. Me and Johan are, so far, unable to express this through discourse in any persuade and thought-through way, but we are affected – to the better we sense.

❧

These sounds have been included in the songs and it is a clearly audible (most obviously as part of the track on "Production") and perhaps even palpable layer of the music of *Organizing Rocks*. But it is much more than just industrially inspired rock. The songs describe and depict the field musically, but there are also some going further and narrating less apparently auditory impressions and observations, such as the different human fates, the local aura, including weather (cold) and local culture (cohesive), different moods and insights of the researchers themselves, as well as methodology and theory from a musical perspective. All three albums express something unique about the field, different aspects of being there. They convey feelings and moods in a way which is both more direct and literally more moving than any written report would be able to do. What I think is particularly unique is the ability to not just express actual moods and climates, but also reflections and even dreams of the place. One of the dreams I tend to hear in many of the songs, over and over again, especially in songs not so obviously connected to the direct experience of the ethnographic study, such as "Wolfpack" or "Spaceland", is an energy which very strongly makes me think of hope. Or, perhaps "think" is not the right word to adopt, it is much more direct. These songs invite me, as reader and listener, to tie an empathic bond which, who knows, may work if I come to visit Kiruna, as a kind of tuning fork for understanding.

If, for Tommy Jensen and Johan Sandström, rock music is part of the cross-media methodology, which they have developed, based on ethnographic inquiry, other authors, Michael Humphreys, Andrew Brown and Mary Jo Hatch[192,] propose that ethnographic research is, by its very nature, quite close to jazz music. Like jazz musicians, ethnographers constantly engage with a dual quest: of finding one's own tune, identity, and one driven by empathy for the social actors in the field. Ethnographers and jazz musicians work through a similar "conversation" defined by a dynamic balance between oneself and others. They face a similar dilemma of both being "inside" a social situation and at the same time expressing it. The conversation is to a large part improvised, and that is where the main insights also came from – both the ethnographer and the talented jazz musician discover and create something new, a new insight, a new correspondence, outside of hitherto known scripts and theories. They both "search for an identity in the sense of a uniquely personal 'voice' or 'signature' that is characteristically theirs and which differentiates them from others engaged in similar work[193]". They experience a "drive for individuation within a social group[194]" tempered by acceptance by others and social norms. This is basically the rhythmic texture of their work, one which may give birth to compelling music – or tales from the field. Even though ethnography may be written down in a purely textual form, even written ethnography begins with an understanding, an interpretation, of the material which also is based on jazz rhythms – a "continuum of increasing imagination and concentration[195]", involving skills such as intuition, flexibility and creativity. At heart, both ethnography and jazz are performed practices. Being attuned to organization can be, according to the authors, taken literally and bring not just more acute understandings of current practices but also something beyond those – a vision of the "what ifs" and aspirations hidden in the field.

Not just research into organizations, but processes of organizing themselves have been depicted in similarity to music. Mary Jo Hatch[196] speaks of emerging structure in organizing as being dynamically akin to jazz performance. In turbulent times structures collapse and are being liquidated on purpose, as part of outsourcing and re-engineering strategies. However, even under such difficult circumstances people often find a way of working together and relating. These ways are precarious, yet, if the co-operating people know and trust each other, can form sustainable patterns. Like jazz musicians, they can mingle together different temporal experiences, which, by emotional anchors, form structural bonds to work through and from. It is an improvisational form of organizing which relies heavily on abilities that contemporary mainstream organizations neither honour nor develop, such as emotion and intuition.

Finally, music as such may bring insights about organizing which open new ways of seeing the world. Daniel Ericsson is a Swedish organization theorist who has dedicated much of his research and writing to music and organizing, seen as each other's metaphors and reflections. Music helps us to understand organizing and organizing can be carried out for the sake of music. In fact, the cases when the two meet and intertwine can be the most illuminating and mind opening for those interested in organization and in music alike, and maybe not just these two broad categories of people, but the so-called contemporary person. Ericsson's most recent book[197], dedicated to an opera being born, is an example of such an amalgamatic approach. It is, furthermore, written in a dramatic fashion, perhaps even with operatic flair, with voice and space given to the organizers in the field, who speak in their own words and with their own emphases. The actors are a group of people who decide to create an opera theatre in rural Sweden, Småland[198]. Thanks to a serendipity that can only be called operatic, the researcher encounters one of the founders of the project on the train, as he is beginning to conceive of the project (together with a co-founder; they had, in their own words, run into each other). The two men talk and decide to meet again with the project unfolding and acquiring critical mass. In one of the scenes of the book the reader understands that this is actually going to happen, as grand and impossible as it seems, a real, professional opera performance is going to take place in the middle of the dark Swedish forest. Well, not in the forest as such, but in a place as enchanted and unlikely – and yet so very operatic – an old unused factory building. We realize that the conversations have substance behind them, they are not only a record of fanatics of music having regular chats about their majestic dreams. They are all that, but there is something substantial unfolding, too. The author titled his book "composing/influential entrepreneurship" and this is a very good name for the processes we observe as they unfold. The organizers are modest people in modest everyday settings, yet when they speak about opera, their dreams and passions, as well as ambitions and aspirations, soar. In the beginning of the book it is difficult to believe that they are going to pull this off. Then they do and it is not surprising at all. And then we see how the magnificent and incredible performance of Mozart's *The Magic Flute*, quite an achievement seen as a one-off event, turns into a beginning of something more stable and structured. It is not just an operatic performance being born, it is, indeed, an opera theatre, with location, team of co-workers, repertoire and structure. The complexity of the organization explodes from day one and continues to grow. It is not a profit-oriented enterprise, but the economic side is very important; making good opera does not come cheap. A zero budget, fashionable in other artistic circuits, is out of the question. But marketing is also a priority, right from the beginning. Do people living in the area have a "natural need" for something on this scale? And where will the artists come from, this is not an amateur production and no rural garage will be helpful in that respect. Instruments, acoustics, sales of tickets, costumes…The processes are also characterized by tensions and controversies, some of which seem to further and support the creation of the opera rather than, as many mainstream management textbooks would have it, be regarded as pathological and unproductive. By the end of the book, I started to strongly suspect that none of this would have been possible if the organizers were not musicians thinking as musicians and acting together as musicians interact. And that it would have been impossible to observe and note down for someone not knowledgeable in and passionately dedicated to music. But then, the author is also a firm believer that music has the power to change societies[199], echoing Jacques Attali, the French economist and advisor to President Mitterrand and himself a president for the European Bank for Reconstruction and Development. Attali considered the area of music and musical industry as both formative and enlightening as of broad societal changes. Music changes the world and tells the story of societal change.

To me, this has always been the case of rock music. The first song that did that for me was Led Zeppelin's "Kashmir", which I heard at my friend's place when I was 12. It was literally like opening a door to another world. I did not understand the lyrics then or know more about the origins of the song than that it was "something Indian", but I could both feel and see before me scenes from an ancient, mythical time, which, much later, made a perfect click together with Bhagavad Gita but perhaps even more with Hermann Hesse's Siddhartha. The song transported me into a realm I would immediately fall in love with and to which I still am dedicated, even though it has now been fiercely unfashionable for years – the Imagination. I have been able to find inspirations and ideas relating to organization and management in that realm, if usually not in music itself but mainly in narratives, myths and poetry, but I am aware that it was music that originally let me into it. Music is particularly able to do it, because it has the ability to move the listener so directly and immediately, almost from inside of the psyche. Quite often one even carries it inside, tunes or melodies that persist in the inner ear. Pieces of music bring back memories almost as closely as if they were being lived again. There are moments in life that are connected with musical tracks which may work as keys to unlock the past. Usually these are moments of grief or joy, love, liberation, sudden epiphanic experiences, rejection, death. But it also happens that they bring back memories of work and organizing. Such is the case of Ray Charles' "Hit the road, Jack", which brings back memories of collective resistance at my workplace when I was a student in Sweden. The radio was playing that tune when a few of us, working at a restaurant, decided that enough was enough, we were not going to wear those high-heeled shoes that our boss instructed us to. We decided to leave the dishes unwashed and contacted the unions. Every time I hear the song, the rebellious mood bubbles up under my skin, anger and the exquisite consolation of collective resistance. We were successful in our protest then. I continue feeling grateful to Ray Charles for it.

Yiannis Gabriel is another organization theorist inspired by music in his thinking. He is currently writing a book about opera and management, where he elaborates on the topic and gives many examples. At the time of my writing this text, it is not yet completed, but there are blog[200] entries and articles available, such as one taking up the lessons about romance and the strife of leadership to be learned from opera[201]. The opera is a highly political genre, not just in its narrative aspect, but in the purely musical – the chorus has the ability to "voice to multitudes of people by means of the chorus and its adeptness at deploying music to enhance, qualify, question or stigmatize what is expressed in the words[202]". The music can open new understandings of dimensions to leadership that are not obvious and sometimes perhaps even not at all possible to grasp through narratives. Far from being the elitist artform it so often is taken for nowadays, opera has historically been able to move people to play, as it was often inspiring popular or even street art, as well as to revolution, which was rather often its theme, and has also happened to be its outcome. Gabriel tells the story of the performance of Auber's opera *La Muette de Portici* in Brussels, which resulted in a crowd storming the local courthouse, which was the beginning of the revolution that led to the independence of Belgium. Opera is often explicitly used to express political ideas of the time, such as nationalism or romanticism. There are also examples of political leaders reacting allergically and violently to performances, such as was the case with Dmitri Shostakovitch's opera *Lady Macbeth of the Mtsensk District* which Stalin himself condemned, not for its narrative, but explicitly for the way it sounded to him. Opera is, concludes Gabriel, "a political phenomenon, not merely in its content but in the passions that it arouses and the political processes it sets in motion[203]". Leadership is, unsurprisingly, one of the themes and archetypes that tends to come up in operatic work, historically and today. The operatic chorus is able to express many collective moods, including the kind of followership that makes a certain leadership style become real or even "inevitable" in a certain period of time. Operas also portray leaders but the roles offered to them are rarely victorious and usually tragic and doomed. Destiny tends to play a central role in many operatic works dedicated to leadership, and the human side is represented as moral conflict and torment. According to Gabriel, opera is able to express the complexity of leadership better than other media, showing the interplay of different forces and vectors and recognizes that it must be a ground of strife and contention. It cannot be rationally measured out, dispersed or programmed, as it plays itself out in several very powerful domains of culture and psyche simultaneously. It also reveals conflict as the core of leadership.

3. Water daily

History
History and presence

History as an academic discipline is the study of the past, as documented and described in documents and other reliable sources. The etymology of the word derives from the Greek expression for inquiry and it is in this sense that it has been used by philosophers such as Aristotle. Herodotus, a Greek author from the fifth century BCE, is often named among the first historians, dedicated to a methodical (and just narrative) study of the past. Cicero referred to him as the father of history and his *Histories*[204] is a ground-breaking account of events and customs taking place in areas around the Mediterranean. His motivation for writing this work was to provide a record for the "great and marvellous deeds"[205] of Greeks as well as barbarians so that they will not be forgotten. He seems to have been aware of the existence of different accounts and sometimes provides several, yet does not keep an uninterested and impartial standpoint. Some of the stories are clearly not factual, but resemble more myths or legends than factographic narratives. However, many of his accounts have been later at least partially confirmed by research and he remains a respected source for modern historians. The narrative contains many dramatic stories, tales about characters, dramatizations of events and vivid exchanges between historical protagonists. His kings, queens and heroes speak and argue, tell stories, explain in a style that is partly embellished, but partly lifelike, if almost certainly not exactly accurate. Even if not a faithful record of what has been said and by whom, it rests a powerful and trustworthy account of a culture.

A much more recent author and historian, celebrated perhaps as much as criticized, is the German philosopher George Friedrich

Hegel. In his lectures published posthumously as the *Philosophy of History*[206] he proposes that there are three approaches to history writing. Original historians, like Herodotus and Thucydides, are those as if natural authors, "whose descriptions are for the most part limited to deeds, events, and states of society, which they had before their eyes, and whose spirit they shared"[207]. Reflective history is written from a distance, "whose spirit transcends the present"[208]. They are much more refined and able to be universal, pragmatic or critical. The most sophisticated approach is philosophical history: the most thoughtful, aiming to find the sense and the ideas driving the events and beliefs. Only from the point of view of history understood this way, is it possible to truly understand and judge what has been unravelling. This distance allows us to see beyond appearances and contingencies and come into contact with what Hegel calls the Spirit, the *Geist:* a dynamic sum of culture, the thrust of its development. The Spirit, which contains intelligence and will, leads to truth, which is, in itself, liberating, like coming closer to God. Human history is the manifestation of this Spirit.

Walter Benjamin, the most contemporary of the three authors, also held a spiritual view of history, albeit in a different sense. To Benjamin[209] ideas can be redeemed and nothing is lost to history. The radical historian can bring everything back to life by disconnecting the story of the victors, pushing aside the obvious to liberate the messianic moments hidden below the surface of the dead, linear time. Liberation is encapsulated in these moments, of which real life is made up: filled, immediate, experienced. The past is never quite gone: it is waiting to be set free by the re-reading of history:

> nothing that has ever happened should be regarded as lost for history. To be sure, only a redeemed mankind receives the fullness of its past – which is to say, only for a redeemed mankind has its past become citable in all its moments.[210]

Redemption lies dreaming in "every second of time was the strait gate through which the Messiah might enter"[211]. Revolution is a kind of transubstantiation, where dead, empty time is transformed into lived qualitative time. Telling the story once again, while looking through the surface, through linear time, for moments that are ready to spring alive and open not just a new future but an entirely different past for us to inhabit.

In the early 1990s, just after the Berlin Wall came down, I was taking my first steps as an organizational ethnographer. I was visiting Berlin just a few years after the big event for a scholarship at the Wissenschaftszentrum. Among other things, I took part in the work of the group studying Berlin as a cultural script. We watched Wim Wenders' *Himmer über Berlin* together and discussed it in research seminars. There are so many ways to see the film, I discovered then, and I still do, when I present it to my students. But that was Berlin and die Mauer was still very intensely present (even if it was not the topic of the film). My colleagues taught me to see Berlin as the film depicts it: as a palimpsest where everything exists all at the same time. We explored different parts of the city together, or I walked alone and talked about my findings with one of my friends from the research group. Nothing was devoid of meaning, everything deserved of stories and I heard an abundance of tales that seemed to be as alive as the many construction sites of the city. There were painful stories and funny ones, sometimes attached to the very same streets, the very same buildings. I thought I almost saw the place where Harry Haller saw the door with the sign that read "Magic Theatre – For Madmen Only – Price of Admission – Your Mind"[212], the streets lost and found in Rainer Fassbinder's films. I walked daily with Walter Benjamin, completely unsurprised when, one evening, an older woman I had never met before gave me a long-stemmed rose. It started to snow and it had a sparkling aura of frost on top of the petals. It did not survive until the morning, even though I did everything

I could to take care of it. It did not wither or wilt. It sort of faded away.

Organizational history

History is, in organization and management studies as well as in other areas, a disciplined approach to the past[213]. It requires the use of multiple scholarly sources, a critical discussion of cited sources, the use of chronological organization of knowledge, and the presence of historiography, that is, the discussion of the methods of historical scholarship and their satisfactoriness. It is a potentially enlightening approach to the area in several important ways.

Firstly, studying history can bring perspective. One of the seminal books on labour and management published in the twentieth century was Harry Braverman's *Labour and Monopoly Capital*[214]. It unravels the tale of the degradation of work since the beginnings of the industrial era, and especially with the introduction of the ideas known as "scientific management" and their spread from the shop floor to office work (and, may I add, currently to everything, including academia). Contemporary management is the effect of the desire to control the production process which is characteristic of capitalism, based on a highly biased and even distorted model of the human being, known as homo economicus, the human being pursuing only self-interest and nothing more. In order to make such a system work, the human has to be directed and pressed into this mould, made to conform to it by systematically excluding all behaviour that transgresses it. Firstly, this is done by the division of the labour process, which should not be confused with the social division of labour, something existing in all societies at all times. Capitalism relies on an artificial management technique which divides the production process into small, multiple tasks, which are easy to perform and control. The worker is paid less for his or her work, which demands much less skill and the responsibility for planning and making sure the work results in an adequate end product is moved upwards in the hierarchy. This knowledge is then monopolized as management. The coordination and planning at the societal level are also systematically passed over to corporate management which tries to transform everything it deals with using the same logic and relying on market mechanisms. Another influential research-based book on management of the last century was also a history book, Roy Jacques' *Manufacturing the Employee*[215]. The book offers a thorough and philosophical reflection on the history of industrial work relations, including sociological, cultural and political contexts and ideas. The book goes back to pre-managerial times of the emergence of big industrial organizations, showing how they influenced the first theories and prescriptions of what management was and what it should achieve. The employee is a cultural construct which can be understood in a historical context, a social role central for the development of the industrial society, organized around several disciplining institutions such as depersonalization of relationships, quantification as replacement for trust and reductionist rationalization. These institutions have been normalized and appear as "normal" or even "inevitable" but they are neither of these things. Jacques shows their historical origin and points to alternative possibilities throughout the book. The last chapter bears the title "The struggle of memory against forgetting: managerialist thought as a conceptual prison"[216]. It explains how these management institutions and ideas have slipped into common sense but do not, in fact, belong in the category of "human condition". A historically informed examination is able to shed light on how they came to pose as necessities and also point out directions of possible alternative development. The currently dominating organization models are dysfunctional and *"the very structure of industrial, corporate-capitalist organizing is based on an addictive understanding of experience in the world"*[217], assuming that growth is imperative and progress means seeking the greatest possible wealth. It was clear for the author writing in the mid-1990s that this was a dead end; nowadays it is even a dangerous, wasteful approach, threatening to put an end to human civilization and maybe to the whole planet we inhabit. Old questions about values, motivation and leadership can be re-framed and reconsidered, instead of continuing to "hammering on intractable and/or irrelevant issues"[218]. The models and artefacts that have ceased to work or are creating more unsolvable problems than solutions to existing ones should be seen as temporary formations.

Perhaps by querying the historical basis of our own common sense we can increase our 'wisdom to know the difference'.[219]

Secondly, history opens our eyes to the falsity of the assumptions regarding the dynamics of management[220]. There is a dominating teleological argument which is a trivialization of history presenting the development as a quasi-natural evolution of organization and management. Mainstream textbooks use it to make the point of the inevitability and superiority of contemporary institutions and present them without interpretation, as if they are a fact of nature. However, more rigorous historical knowledge brings immediately to attention that many of these "facts" are no more than interpretations. Some, such as the well-known Theory X and Y are, furthermore, currently read against their original intent: in this case, it was to invite a discussion about authority in organizations. Historical reflection brings back life and inquisitive power to many theories and ideas, as well as the many possibilities still present in the body of knowledge once we have freed them from the "procrustean transformation", which limits theory and practice to the same range of solutions.

Thirdly, thanks to historical analysis we are able to see more clearly the contribution of some strands of thought about organization and management. For example, organizational development (OD) is one of the most central approaches to organizational change but there is much confusion about its usefulness and durability[221]. Adopting a historical analysis helps to discern its origin, namely participative management and action research, as well as driving dynamics, which has for a long time been the desire to acquire more workplace democracy. Only at a later stage did profit take overhand over people and transformative change became the most popular mode of managing organizational dynamics. By taking into consideration the extensive body of historical knowledge it is now possible to strive for the development of more humane and humanistic ideas of change. Historical analysis also helps to reclaim the missing voice from a strand of thought in management theory and make the whole theory more scientifically wholesome and less ideologically biased by redressing the balance. For example, the contribution of the left which has been written out of management history and OD[222]. The discourse has been writing its own history in a way that has in recent years concealed the significant contribution that people and ideas of the left have had in the development of some of the key concepts, such as group dynamics and action research. Yet change management is not ideologically neutral and the current managerialist takeover can be undone or at least undermined by a historical analysis.

> Historiographical processes, the way that history comes to be written, the choices made in selecting and ignoring past events, are shaped by prevailing, albeit competing, societal power relations and the associated ideologies[223].

The writing of history is ideological, but awareness and historiography: contrasting accounts and sources, may bring back clarity and once again bring back ideas and concepts to discussion and possible re-interpretation.

Finally, history helps to see and appreciate the peripheries that are less visible in the extremely colonially minded mainstream management science (and practice). Polish organizational historiographers Tomasz Ochinowski and Michał Szukała[224] present a consciously radical programme of a reflectively marginal writing of the history of Polish organizations, on its own terms, using Polish sources and comparing them with American narratives. Such focus cannot only help us to understand the current context of organizing better, but bring to light truths and lessons for the centre to be learned from peripheries. For example, the Polish narratives unveil valid implications about social aspects of entrepreneurship which stood out in the analysed material in the form of intensive relationships with institutions of the state and with important (aristocratic) elites. The Polish original entrepreneur was a social character, with roots in trade (not small services as in the American myth). In a book dedicated to Polish business history and historiography, Tomasz Ochinowski[225] engages with the rich cultural heritage, particularly the Łódź region, where Catholic, Jewish and other traditions have been intensively mixing and particularly in the area of business and entrepreneurship. The author believes that understanding history can be enlightening for making contemporary organizations more vital and sustainable. It also enables seeing the past as part of the immediate context, which can help in finding "roads less walked" and opportunities unused. It is something of a recycling of ideas; a respectful approach to local identities and traditions and making good use of the traditions held by communities of people.

I asked Roy Jacques for a reflection on the uses of history and he came up with the following essay.

Roy Jacques: History, why?

Perhaps the best-known product of my academic career has been *Manufacturing the Employee*, a discursive history of "the employee" – a nineteenth-century production of industrializing America and the taken-for-granted subject of Business School dogma. That I took the so-called "historic turn" in organization studies at all, let alone more than a decade before such a turn was articulated, is, as one might currently say, a serious WTF?

I did not train as a historian. I entered doctoral study as an MBA from a software management career hoping to make a concrete, practical contribution to management and organizing based on (1) my work experience and (2) my belief that making organizations more humane and making organizations more effective are synergistic, not competing, goals. In the late 1980s when I was doing my dissertation work, there was intense buzz about post-industrial organizations and the emerging challenge of managing the so-called "knowledge workers" who would putatively be the driving force of "knowledge-intensive organizations" in the emerging "knowledge society". Looking at what was then the dogma of my field – the management textbooks, the "classic" studies, the popular management bookshelf, the pundits and towering figures of the discipline – I found little that was relevant to my experience as either an employee or a manager and much that was counterproductive. In retrospect, I have often said that should Ford call to ask the field to consult on how to operate the River Rouge plant (opened in 1928), there are several important questions relevant to them that are on the verge of being answered today...

Additionally, fundamental to the dogma of my field was a faith-based belief that when important questions will be answered they will be answered only by the accumulated statistical significance of quantitatively tested hypotheses because the management disciplines are imminently becoming a paradigmatic scientific discipline. As my work background was statistical financial forecasting, the numbers were familiar to me, but they didn't answer any of the questions I was asking. Thus I came to be ontologized as a qualitative researcher (and a radical). I have never sworn allegiance to numbers, words or Kropotkin. I am a researcher, period. I use numbers and words as tools and when a question I ask can be answered with a binary yes/no obtainable from hypotheticodeductive quantification, I will not hesitate to torture the numbers until they confess.

Three decades ago, the dawn of post-industrial organizing was commonly claimed to represent the greatest change in the world of work since industrialization. If so, I thought, the rush at that time to produce a prescriptive literature about managing post-industrial employees by appending modifications to the existing literature was both superficial and premature, since the management disciplines themselves were produced *de novo* around the problems of industrialization. This was clear from the topics, approaches and solutions proffered by the core dogma of the discipline. The central conflict I saw between the boundaries of the knowledge base as it existed and emerging problems in tech situations with which I had experience was this: *"Management" was* (and remains) *primarily a discourse about obtaining worker* **compliance** *while the central problem of mobilizing knowledge in complex organizations requires the ability to manage worker* **initiative**.

"Management", then, was not an open field of inquiry within which to pose any problem of organizing. It was itself a problem to solve, since the emergent issues were not "within the true" of the discipline. They could not be articulated, let alone explored. Further, the governing narrative of the discipline was that, beginning in the late nineteenth century (which coincides with the problems of US industrialization), scientific study of work created a foundation of Truth upon which future researchers have built and upon which we must keep building. This narrative commits the field to a discourse of worker control and the supremacy of the exceedingly narrow knowledge claim of the tested, quantitative hypothesis.

The motivation for my historical work was to show that the

problem of the "knowledge worker" was more analogous to the shift from Ptolemaic to Galilean astronomy than it was to the tower-building of King Nimrod. Just as it took two generations to produce, accept and understand "the employee", producing the knowledge worker would not be an overnight task. A new object of knowledge was emerging.

I was neither after the Truth about the past nor was I interested in the past for voyeuristic reasons. The task, as I saw it, was to show the situated roots of management discourse – the (largely American) culture from which it arose, the problems of the time, the interests represented in articulating which problems would count, the power relationships and politics behind the narrow pseudo-scientificity required for credibility as an expert. This was not an attack on the discipline, but an attempt to bound it as having developed to solve certain problems whose relevance was passing. Only by first coming to see the accumulated knowledge of the field in this way could discursive space be cleared for knowledge more relevant to situations dependent on worker initiative than to the worker-compliant past of River Rouge. This work is still only in its earliest stages.

Mythical stories
Myths for the profane

Myths are stories referring to sacred spheres. Other narratives touching profound symbolism but pertaining to the profane, I propose to call archetypical tales[226]. In this book I focus on the intersection between the sacred and the profane, so I will be talking about mythical stories. I will first explain how I understand myth, and then briefly address the fundamental symbolic component of mythical narratives, archetypes.

Ernst Cassirer[227] understood myths as a language, full of symbols and metaphors, used to describe spiritual reality or the religious experiences that cannot be expressed in ordinary words. The language of myths abounds in symbols and metaphors.

In colloquial speech to say that something is a "myth" means that it is, simply put, false, a lie, or perhaps a misconception or false belief. For Roland Barthes[228] (and in literary theory and constructivist philosophy) myth is a semiological system, a kind of speech expressing the dominant ideology and serving to naturalize the social order in the interests of the ruling classes. The way that I will be using the term is not rooted in colloquial language or on semiologic tradition, but based on an anthropological and narrativistic view, which regards myth as an expression of a truth beyond the material reality. It is not relevant whether a mythical story accurately describes events that had really taken place. The important issue is if it touches a deeper spiritual truth and narrates:

> matters fundamental to ourselves, enduring essential principles about which it would be good for us to know; about which, in fact, it will be necessary for us to know if our conscious minds are to be kept in touch with our own most secret, motivating depths. In short, these holy tales and their images are messages to the conscious mind from quarters of the spirit unknown to normal daylight consciousness, and if read as referring to events in the field of space and time – whether of the future, present, or past – they will have been misread and their force deflected, some secondary thing outside then taking to itself the reference of the symbol, some sanctified stick, stone, or animal, person, event, city, or social group[229].

Joseph Campbell[230] explains that myths connect two realities: the external and the internal. The former provides images and symbols, as well as a language and cultural frame that enable us to communicate with others. The latter offers understanding and consciousness that gives sense to all experience, including that of external reality. It does so metaphorically, and should not be taken literally: a literal reading of myths will indeed lead in false or deceptive directions. Their real purpose is to point to fundamental meanings. In this, they resemble art. Karen Armstrong[231] points to the transformative power of both art and myth, direct and experiential. Neither art not myth needs to argue or convince. Both should move, stir, invite to participation. While art may call to partake in testing of new realities, or constructing them, myth summons to take part in something that has existed since times immemorial. In Joseph Campbell's[232] words, it established a link between current and primordial consciousness. It provides a link between the non-material reality and the embodied one. In doing so, it inspires respect, reverence, deference for the cosmos and creation, by letting people experience something larger than themselves. It validates a certain sociological system, its order, norms and values. Finally, the role of myth is to guide the person through different stages of life.

Mythical narratives, both sacred and profane, contain one further element, unique in its kind, more powerful than symbols or metaphors. What makes them resonate so strongly with the psyche are archetypes. Carl Gustav Jung[233] saw them as empty slots, reminiscent of riverbeds, ready to hold images, symbols and plots, which are located in the collective unconscious. He did not present a uniform theory of archetypes, and his views were evolving continuously. However, the main point is that archetypes are universal and open, and able to attract meaning. They inspire new ideas and interpretations, and some of those never age, despite the passage of time, and make profound sense to people from different cultures. So it is with art that relies on them, such as Shakespeare's plays, Greek myths and classical Chinese poetry. Archetypes as such are neither good nor bad; they all have both a light and a dark side. They never replace judgement or conscience, rather, they provoke to deep thought and unsettle, bringing to mind truths beyond the easy and the common sense. They can be said to be the exact opposite to stereotype. They are doors connecting humans to larger meanings.

It always seems to us as if meaning – compared with life – were the younger event, because we assume, with some justification, that we assign it of ourselves, and because we believe, equally rightly no doubt, that the great world can get along without being interpreted. But how do we assign meaning? From what source, in the last analysis, do we derive meaning? The forms we use for assigning meaning are historical Categories that reach back into the mists of time – a fact we do not take sufficiently into account. Interpretations make use of certain linguistic matrices that are themselves derived from primordial images. From whatever side we approach this question, everywhere we find ourselves confronted with the history of language[234].

Archetypes exist simultaneously in two spaces: the intersubjective, common to all human beings, and the inner spiritual space.

Organizational mythmaking

My grandmother Weronika liked telling tales: about books she's read, people she's met, films she's seen. Also folk tales from the region where she was born and grew up in a farmer's family. I loved her stories, both the true ones and the fairy tales. One of my great favourites was a traditional story of the man who is walking back home from the market. It is late and he has to walk all alone through the forest. He is young and completely unafraid – for what is there to be scared of? After all, he knows his way very well and he is no weakling. Rather, it is the other men in the village who look up to him for his courage and fitness. And it is not yet dark. So he walks straight ahead. Then, suddenly, he sees something lying in his path. It's red and not very big – a shoe! A woman's leather boot, very pretty, but only one of them. He lifts it up to look at but puts it down again. What is the use of just one shoe, however red and pretty? He walks on. And then, he sees something red on the path…he comes closer and yes, it's a shoe, a lovely red shoe, and it looks like it's the other one of the pair. "Oh no," he thinks, "if I had only taken the first, I'd had two of them now!" He looks at the shoe. He looks up above the treetops. It's not that late yet! He takes the shoe and turns around, back to where he'd seen the first of the pair. But when he gets to the point, it's gone! He looks and looks, checks the bushes, decides that it must have been further back, as he sees no footsteps other than his own. He must have made a mistake! The shoe was lying somewhere else. He continues to walk but it's nowhere to be seen. He sighs deeply and turns around again. Leaving the second shoe – what's the use of just one shoe, after all? He walks on and on, it keeps getting darker. Then, he sees something lying on the ground. A penny – just a little penny, lying in the dust. But now he is in a hurry, and he thinks: dammit! No, I'm not stopping here in the middle of the forest, it's just one silly penny, worth nothing, the single shoe must have been worth more than that! You see, he was just a peasant boy, but farmers in our region were not poor, they owned their land and valued work more than they valued things or coins. He just marches on, longing to see his wife and children, for whom he carried sweeties from the market. But after having walked for a longish time, he sees something lying on the ground. Another penny! He lifts it up, looks at it with much regret. For a penny is nothing, but two pennies, well, that's quite another thing! Two pennies can buy a candy for the kid or a stopping of tobacco pipe for himself. What a pity! He thinks, so silly of me not to have taken that first one! He looks up at the sky, it's getting dark now. Then at the penny in his hand. He shrugs. "Why not! This will not take long." And he turns back to look for the first penny. But when he gets to the place where it had laid, it is no longer there! He looks around, he gets down on his knees to check if it's not buried in the sand. Alas, it is nowhere to be found. He jumps up, angry, and throws the lonely penny away, swearing nastily: "May the devil take you, damned thing!" and when he does this, he hears a slight noise somewhere in the darkness, as if a muffled snigger. He stands still and listens: no, it must have been an illusion. And he turnsaround yet again and walks back, towards home. It is very dark now and the forest makes all kinds of noises. He sees things in the distance, like glittering eyes. Then a sight makes him stop abruptly: a hangman. He is hanging, dangling from a tree. He looks quite dead. "Nothing I can help with here", he says to himself, "I must go and I must go really fast, or I will not get back home before midnight. Or worse…" He crossed himself and keeps on walking. And then, suddenly, no! Not another one! Yet another hangman. He stops to pray. The man looks quite dead. This is not good at all. He should not have left the first one like that, it was a man, he should not have left him like an animal. Reluctantly, he turns around and walks back all the way to where the first hangman had been. But when he arrives, he is nowhere to be seen. No trace, nothing. Only a sound of cracking and as if something snapping in the darkness. He is very tired and very much afraid now, but he knows that he cannot stop, he must keep on walking. So he turns around and continues on his way home, though the darkness and the moving shadows of the forest. When he finally reaches his village, it is getting light again, the sun is about to rise. He knows that he is safe now, but something terrifying has planted itself in his dreams.

I was always equally terrified but also mesmerized by this story and I kept asking my grandmother: what happened, why was he seeing all these things? My grandmother said: the devil was deceiving him to get lost in the forest. Not until much later did I learn what Freud and Bettelheim wrote about the meaning of fairy tales, how the dreamlike and uncanny is being spun into tales to carry sense that is at the same time profoundly human and not quite expressible in everyday, rational speech. I also learned about pattern recognition, something that always has been extremely important to me: I like thinking in terms of patterns, and two is, for me, the beginning of a meaningful configuration. My friends sometimes admonish me for spinning realities from two stray coincidences and I have to watch myself when I interpret ethnographic material: it is an urge to jump into premature conclusions and it should be resisted most of the time. But it works well for me when I write poetry. Poetry is sometimes about jumpstarting worlds from insufficient evidence. They do not unravel like in novels, but, when they are any good, they flutter. This is, perhaps, why this fairy tale always made such a massive impression on me and I preferred it to all the other fantastic stories that my grandmother used to tell me, about talking roosters, smart countrywomen, devils that in their heart of hearts quite liked humans and sometimes stood up for the underdogs, and silly youngest sons who then turned out to be both wise and good. They were all great stories, but the one about the man lost in the forest had planted itself in my dreams.

Organization theorist Martin Bowles[235] uses Greek myths to show the profound importance of communication in organizations. Ancient gods and goddesses embody the values and virtues that are important for an organization but are impossible to be unambiguously codified. It is not advisable to try doing so, as it would drain them of their deeper meaning and turn them into either shallow bubbles of regulation or into oppressive systems of domination. Yet seen as archetypical roles, they retain the power to at the same time communicate important values and invite into serious enactment. For example, Zeus symbolizes the hierarchical order, based on personal power. Both the leader inspired by Zeus and his or her organization base are immersed in a culture of power and emotional distance. In contrast, an Apollonian organization is bureaucratic and concerned with law and regulations: a culture of transparency and law. Athena inspires strategically minded leaders and organizations, concerned with pragmatism and rationality. But inspiration also has a dark side, represented by gods such as Poseidon, Aries and Hades. They are constantly present in our cultural mind frame and, if made conscious, can symbolize energies such as creativity, competitiveness and mystery. However, they are often repressed in contemporary organizations and turn destructive, bringing forth dark and violent behaviour. Bowles notes that some Olympians tend to be absent from modern organizations: the goddesses of home, family and the female side, Demeter, Aphrodite and Artemis. This says something about contemporary management perhaps as eloquently as the overrepresented gods, such as Zeus and Athena. Organizations often are dominated by mythical characters linked to power and manipulation, but fail to represent the vast spectrum of human feelings and values.

What is absent from the conscious sphere of communication does not disappear but makes up an unconscious force, the organization shadow[236]. It is the dark side of the organization that develops in obscurity and sometimes explodes with immense, destructive strength, astonishing and terrifying people – the observers and even the participants themselves. The paradox is that the more management tries to control and steer the organization's culture, the better the growing ground for the shadow side. It thrives on power, domination and suppression. Striving for perfection but unable to perceive its limitations, such organizations lose the ability to see their mistakes. Managers project negative signals on others: competitors, clients, trade unions, their own scapegoated employees. Employees tend to feel uneasy, depressed, with time depressed, terrified and desperate. The culture turns on its own participants by a system of entanglement, oppression and manipulation, which usually prompts management to employ even more control, regulations and procedures. A vicious circle makes the leadership and the communicative system increasingly toxic and sinister. The only measure to solve this problem is to confront the weaknesses and negativity. Only the light of consciousness can defeat the darkness of the shadow.

Another strong voice for engaging with darkness is that of Yiannis Gabriel[237], one of the most original and interesting authors using myth as epistemological metaphor to explain existential aspects of organizations, who applies the ancient Greek idea of *miasma* to describe an infectious state of pollution, which is at the same time material, psychological, moral and spiritual, which affects people in some organizations. It occurs in organizations undermining people's self-confidence and dignity and focusing on an idealized and perfectly rational image. People are criticized and objectified, communication becomes stifled and devoid of humour and warmth. There is a physical sense of contamination:

> People frequently complained of breathing difficulties, headaches and other physical symptoms, which they attributed to the hot and stagnant air and the failure of the air-conditioning system. For prolonged periods, a putrid smell pervaded the building, caused by faulty sewerage pipes and blocked drains, contributing to a sense of failure and decay.[238]

The newly employed often think that this does not pertain to them and hope to be able to steer clear of the atmosphere of the workplace. However, this turns out to be as good as impossible. The discussions, which circle around blame and uncleanliness, have a most invasive character, penetrating to people's subconscious minds, and having an outcome in dreams about inadequacy and shame. People feel compelled to spend an increasing amount of time at the premises of the organization, but do not feel they perform any meaningful work. Simultaneously the organizational culture runs dry of stories.

Sounds organizations are alive with stories and managers are dedicated storytellers. In an organization touched by miasma this ability seems to disappear. The organization becomes overtaken by melancholia, intense sense of loss, vilification of the past and disconnection with it, and feelings of individual failure. Managerial efforts to control and cleanse often have the opposite effect and only lead to even more pollution of this kind. Another typical measure undertaken by organizations polluted by miasma is scapegoating, which may alleviate the sense of doom for a time but does not solve the problem, either. What instead can help the organization is making conscious what is hidden in such cultures, and here myth can help to bring it to light and describe in words. In Greek myth miasma is a toxic state touching groups and communities of people as a result of an offence to something divine. For example, Oedipus brings miasma to Thebes because of him having killed his father and married his mother, even though he was not aware of doing so. It spreads like Black Death, not sparing anyone, neither guilty nor innocent. One of the most perplexing features is the lack of resistance it meets, as if it affected resistance itself. Organizations touched by miasma become total institutions, occupying whole life-worlds of their participants. Miasma, to be cured, has to be recognized and atoned for. The first step of atonement is profound mourning, learning from myth that instructs how to embrace intense and conscious mourning, acknowledging the wrongs that have been done, embracing the guilt but rejecting the shame.

In my book *Organizations and Archetypes*[239] I talk about both the important absences and the significant presences in organizations that can be best expressed by invoking archetypes and mythical tales. I present selected classical archetypes of the development of the self, such as the shadow and the persona, and of social roles, such as the king, the sage and the trickster against the broader background of myths, art and traditional tales. Then

I explore the occurrence of archetypical tales relating to these archetypes, more or less directly, in organization theory and practice. All of them have both a light and a dark side and one cannot be understood fully without the taking into consideration of the other. They have enormous significance for organizational cultures, potential for creativity and renewal, but, if not engaged with consciously, may have a destructive effect on organizations and their participants. If brought into the light of conscious communication, organizational archetypes may activate the collective imagination to genuine creativity and insight. This is important if we are to create a sustainable organizational future to replace the current dysfunctional system based on an almost total eclipse of meaning and purpose by financial measures and aims, seriously endangering the survival of the natural and cultural context. The book proposes a new, humanistic management to draw ideas from tradition and a broader cultural frame of reference. This is where the archetypes can play a key role, signalling recurring vital themes and highlighting key questions.

> In that broad frame of reference, management is about techniques and skills, not a purely economic function, but a kind of uniting service to the managed organization, which I conceive of…as similar to that of poets and artists to their communities of thought. But managers, unlike poets and artists, do not have their own Muse. Therefore they have to learn from these traditionally creative groups or, through archetypes, look for a Muse of their own.[240]

Finally, entire organizations are sometimes mythologized and granted an extraordinary, nearly sanctified status. They acquire supernatural qualities, such as serving as the symbol for a country, as in the case of IKEA of Sweden; quintessence of a virtue: solidity as in the case of Mercedes; holder carrier of supernatural abilities: like has happened with the CIA. Quite often certain organizational skills, abilities or attributes are mythologized, such as grandeur, leadership or pioneering. Some organizational roles, such as, notably, managers and entrepreneurs, are endowed with heroic attributes and become objects of mythologization[241]. It also happens that organizations become immortalized or thought to be immortal, god-like and a kind of substitute for collective spirituality. This happens especially in rationalistic, tightly managed organizations, which deny not only their soul but suppress collective feelings. Burkard Sievers[242] argues that this happens not because of employment of active imagination but by the emergence of an important absence in the superficial management culture: the absence of death from mainstream organizational discourses. The organization then becomes a symbolic stand-in for the immortal soul of its participants and appears as a powerful (even if internally dead) divinity. The example of the collective megalomania called the Third Reich comes to mind: many people really believed it was immortal and a vehicle to carry their own human and spiritual significance. It was a cause for many Germans to genuinely and fanatically believe in. As extreme as this example may be, it points to the central issue: managers often prefer the illusory certainty granted by organizations to the engagement with real spirituality. The reason why this happens so often is not just the incompetence of current management to handle spiritual issues but is related to power. It is easy to accumulate power by deification of the organization. This kind of empty deity requires sacrifices of individuality, emotions, passions and agency. In return employees partake in illusory immortality and the founders try to immortalize themselves through their firms and brands. Organizations are somewhat like the Olympians: they only take but do not give blessings in exchange.

I would like to end this section with a suitable tale – a version of the legend of the Grail[243]. As it happens, this youngest among

King Arthur's knights, was the one who first found the Grail. He found it only to lose it again. And this is what took place on that fateful day and night. Perceval met the Wounded King who invited him to stay the night at his castle. During a sumptuous dinner organized in his honour, he observes astounding and truly astonishing things. A procession of youths carry strange and powerful artefacts. Then a beautiful young girl enters carrying the Grail itself. It is so brilliant that all the surrounding lights appear dim and faint. It is made of gold and precious stones of incomparable beauty. The procession goes by him and leaves the room. All that surpasses his imagination and leaves him speechless. By the way, he had been taught not to talk too much, as it does not befit a knight. So he says nothing, dazzled and petrified, and after the dinner, he goes to sleep. Only later he learns that he should have asked questions, engaged in a conversation about all the amazing symbols he saw. Then the King and his barren land would have been healed and the Grail would have become his. But he did not speak, he could not, lacking a language and a mindset for such unusual things. So instead, he wakes up the next day, alone. The Grail is gone, and so is the King, and indeed, the castle. He lies wide awake with his head resting on a stone.

It is important to be able to talk about the important things in our lives, also in organizational life, because organizations are so crucial in our times. All the significant things, sometimes strange, sometimes terrifying, beautiful, astounding, the procession of symbols before our eyes – let us not remain speechless before them, as not to wake up in the midst of a wasteland with a stone for a pillow under our heads. They need to and should be addressed, questions need to be asked; we, organization researchers and participants, need to recognize and talk about the most fundamental issues of what it means to be human and part of a living planet. Only then can we hope for a healing of ourselves and our environment and address some of the most serious and damaging problems of our times. We are not helpless in the face of an impersonal omnipotent Invisible Hand, nor fated to live bleak lives where only standards, quotas, rates, indexes and other figures count, but such things as goodness, happiness, compassion and responsibility are irrelevant because of a lack of language and mindset. This language exists but requires a mindset that has been conspicuously absent from the organizational discourse.

Religion
Kristin Falk Saughau[244]: What is religion good for?

"I do not mind if people think God is a man. But I know for sure that 'God' is a girl's name." This was my 6-year-old son's response when I told him that some people talk about God as a "father". I wish all people could be just as tolerant to the diverse interpretation of God! But religion seems to be the big divide and identity marker in our time. But. We should, I think, look into concepts of religion more as the basic question we all ask into the meanings of our lives. If we do that we might get into a dialogue about our diverse understandings and concepts of what it means to be human. And we should approach religion as a cultural means of understanding these existential questions. Because that is what religion is about. What does it mean to be human, in the deepest sense of the word? Religion is questioning. Without these questions we cease to live fully. We cease to be human. But we are human, and this is what religion can, if addressed with an open mind, remind us about: our humanity.

Religion sustains hope

Religion is a cultural institution relating to the supernatural, including structures, organizations, symbols, places and practices. There are thousands of religions, but a vast majority of the religious population, as well as a predominant majority of the world's population, adhere to one of the main religions of the world: Christianity, Islam, Hinduism or Buddhist. The unaffiliated are either atheists, dedicated non-believers, or agnostics, not wanting to make assumptions about what they consider unknown or unknowable. Academic disciplines dedicated to religion include theology and religion studies. Anthropologist Clifford Geertz defines religion as a:

(1) system of symbols which acts to (2) establish powerful, pervasive, and long-lasting moods and motivations in men by (3) formulating conceptions of a general order of existence and (4) clothing these conceptions with such an aura of factuality that the (5) moods and motivations seem uniquely realistic.[245]

According to Geertz, religion is important because it offers an idea of the world, the self and the relationships between them. In that capacity it serves as a kind of ontological foundation for the creation of culture. Only part of this understanding is metaphysical, the rest relates to a range of experiences and makes them graspable. It serves as a template for interpretation as well as the creation of culture. It is not just a question of what people believe in, but how they cope with the social and psychological, how they make sense of it. Also Karen Armstrong emphasizes this aspect of religion; originally:

religion…was not primarily something that people thought but something they did…[It] is a practical discipline that teaches us to discover new capacities of mind and heart.[246]

It requires perseverance, discipline and dedicated work – some may become better at it, while some will not. Religion still is "like art…an attempt to construct meaning in the face of the relentless pain and injustice of life"[247] and its power lies far beyond the territory of proof and rationality. Religion has to be cultivated and for that purpose different modes of consciousness have to be adopted. This is another characteristic that religion shares with the arts: a linear reliance of the rational reasoning does not suffice for its practitioner. Not all practitioners are able to achieve the higher states, but it is here that some of the religious institutions, most notably art, come to help: for example, the Christian Orthodox faithful can glimpse the mystery in the icons[248], but "just explaining it" does not work and, indeed, makes no sense. Armstrong argues that even if God has been declared dead on many occasions in recent times, unless we insist on trying to make him (or her) graspable and rational, or a fundamentalist simplistic idol, religion is far from a song of the past. Human beings cannot bear meaninglessness, they actively strive to make sense. A great system of meaning that requires a respectful discipline, that is at the heart of religion, has never lost its relevance, even if its structures, assumptions and explanations often have.

Psychologist and philosopher William James believed that religion offers real experiences of fundamental human emotions, regardless of their neurological origins, or manifestations which may seem disconnected from the material life context.

Religious melancholy, whatever peculiarities it may have *quá* religious, is at any rate melancholy. Religion is happiness. Religious trance is trance[249].

To James religious practice is, at least potentially, linked to exercising consciousness, making it possible to come in touch with the rationalistic and superficial aspects of reality. It gives a sense of connection, of relating to something bigger than oneself. James saw religion as a pathway towards spirituality and mysticism, which, for him, was a real knowledge beyond the material. Mysticism is noetic, that is it refers to insights of states of knowledge and truth beyond the discursive intellect.

They may not be translatable into narrative logic, but they bring a stable and endurable sense of revelation and understanding. It comes sporadically and irregularly, but methodical religious practice can welcome it to happen.

Franciscan friar Richard Rohr considers spirituality to be a kind of intense awareness.

> Spirituality is about seeing. It's not about earning or achieving. It's about relationships rather than results or requirements. Once you see, the rest follows[250].

It is an invitation to enlightenment, according to Rohr, but religious institutions, as solid as they may be, cannot guarantee that it ever takes place. It is possible but unpredictable, unpredicted, and cannot be isolated as *something in the mind*. For the religious practitioner, it happens in a context, with others, often – for others. This is the true meaning of "happiness". In the words of Siddhartha Gautama Buddha:

> *Wakefulness is the way to life.*
> *The fool sleeps*
> *As if he were already dead,*
> *But the master is awake*
> *And he lives forever.*
>
> *He watches.*
> *He is clear.*
>
> *How happy he is!*
> *For he sees that wakefulness is life.*
> *How happy he is,*
> *Following the path of the awakened.*
>
> *With great perseverance*

He meditates, seeking
Freedom and happiness.[251]

Consciousness and presence are, for the religious practitioner, not the means but an end in itself, a fundamental truth. Also, awareness does not mean to be *aware of something*, it is a way of being[252]. Awareness is not tied to any object outside of it even if it can be directed towards the Other. It can also be directed inwards, towards silence, towards presence. It is "a view of reality free of ideas and judgements"[253]: when we evaluate, understanding ceases.

But religion and spirituality are not just of being present in the moment as many people seem to think these days (such as the lovely MBA students I had a little chat with about these matters recently; they were more than interested in finding genuine spirituality, but they seemed to believe that it is perfectly possible to acquire it by focusing on the moment). Fr Jeremiah Myriam Shryock from the Community of Franciscan Friars of the Renewal explains in his *Letters of Hope and Consolation*[254] that more is needed. It is important to be aware of God, of others, to be patient and not let the mind be taken over by boredom. One of the key issues is a conscious presence in the context: relationships, other humans, sometimes revealing their good sides and sometimes not, and a realization of the experiences in life, a reclaiming of memory.

One of the greatest dangers in spiritual life is forgetfulness[255].

The world may have become self-obsessed and violent, but spirituality does not mean closing an eye to it; rather, it means being firmly present and to have hope. We are all called to being prophets in these times.

The Friars of Renewal is an interesting and quite alternative organization. It was established in the late 1980s as a community striving to reclaim the original Franciscan ideals, such as poverty, deep spirituality, and solidarity with the dispossessed. I was visiting a good old friend who is a Benedictine monk living in a monastery in the far north, among powerful nature and far away from larger human settlements, as well as from noisy roads and airports. There is a strong feeling of serenity and calm pervading the landscape. My friend tells me sometimes of the animals that are completely unafraid and that come close to him when he is walking in the countryside: the pheasants, badgers, even deer. He came face to face with a swallow once, when he was standing on the bell tower of the church, taking in the scenery. She looked him in the eyes, seemed rather curious and not frightened at all. There is no intrinsic reason why humans, even collectives of humans, should be antagonistic to the natural environment. The aura of the place is one of kindness and slowness, extending through the land, the buildings and the people. I was staying in the pilgrims' cottage a bit away from the monastery and the church. The rhythms of the devotions were not as prevalent in that area, the bells did not quite resonate that strongly, but the pace was just as slow. Maybe that was why I came late to the service on the second day of my stay. I am usually a person who comes too early rather than late and I tend to be in a hurry most of the time. There, I did not. When I entered church, everyone was already sitting and singing. And then a rather amazing thing happened – one of the friars, dressed in a very simple grey dress, turned around and smiled at me with his entire person, as if genuinely happy to see me. We had a chat after Mass and I jokingly told him this was the first time in my life I saw a member of the clergy being happy to see someone coming late to church. He laughed and said he was indeed happy to see me, glad that I came, as well as all the other people attending Mass that day. He explained that he was there on holiday. As a Franciscan Friar of the Renewal he was usually living among the homeless and destitute, often sleeping rough, but even if he was spending the night indoors, he never used a bed, just a mattress. He did all that to be closer to people. He said this made him happy. He laughed a lot, and always seemed to laugh with his entire body. I asked him about the order, what it was like to take part in its work and how he saw its role in the contemporary world. He explained to me that he believed in collaborative effort and that the order was, at the same time, a kind of genuine community, and a directed and organized effort at making a difference: each of the monks individually and all of them together, collectively. Engaging with God and with the world, he said, is how I believe we can make a difference.

Religion has come to be much more prevalent in organization theory in recent years, largely due to the broadening interest in culture, claim Emma Bell and Scott Taylor[256]. The cultural turn "revived managerial interest in exploring the sacred dimension of organizations and drew attention to the religious potential in management"[257]. Culture management in its various guises has led to the emphasis on "emotional links" between employees and work organizations. This has led to an insight that religion is much more important as a frame of thought and understanding for many people than management studies used to realize. This, in turn, made some authors and practitioners consider religion a new territory for management to use and colonize, and so "in terms of both practice and analysis management has at the very least acquired some of the language and characteristics of religion, albeit in a secularized version".[258] The area of "spirituality management" has been attempting to colonize yet another aspect of human life, intruding on issues that used to be private and developing a totalizing discourse. However, simultaneously, there has emerged a strand of theorizing reaching far beyond these tendencies to control and tame religion and spirituality, working in the opposite direction, offering hope and liberation. I will present some general ideas of how religion can fulfil this role in organizations and then give some examples of how concrete religious practices and convictions can help to find meaning beyond neoliberal managerialism.

Religion and organizing

Pater Case, Robert French and Peter Simpson[259] propose a closer historical view on theory, revealing its theological roots and close connection to contemplation, *theoria*. The current tendency to secularize reflection led to the disregarding of what used to be an integral part of theorizing: knowledge of the divine. Even the so-called spiritual management theory lacks and even excludes this knowledge. This limits and severely impoverishes the way we conceive of organizations and the role of humans in them, and reduces everything, including spirituality, to a tool for greater productivity. Reclaiming the connection to the divine offers a radical way out of the impasse. This signifies "eschewal of the instrumental in favour of a more open-ended, ethically disinterested and other-centred disposition toward workplace relations and responsibilities"[260]. *Theoria,* in its original meaning, derived from philosophy and theology, implies seeing, involving vision and intuitive insight and knowing beyond words, connecting with direct experience. With regard to organizations, this would mean recognizing levels of meaning that have been excluded in recent years and allowing for the pursuit and adoption of mystical wisdom. Organizations would make active use of the contemplative position, from which it is possible and legitimate to just experience being alive in the world, without immediate links or imperatives to do something, act out something or achieve some aim. Such an approach would not "necessarily generate knowledge in the modern scientific sense, it might open contemporary minds to an awareness of the relations that exist in the wider community and in the organizations of which they are a part"[261]. This would also bring back a deeper sense of ethics into organizations, as conscience is experienced and not calculated.

As I said earlier, religion cannot only help us to gain such a deeper perspective on organizations, but concrete religions may offer specific insights and ideas. And so, for example, Harro Höpfl[262] muses on the implications for work ethics that can be derived from Catholic Christianity. While the Protestant work ethic is a well-known concept, the Catholic variety may not be so famous. Traditionally, Catholicism was associated with ascetism and obedience. While the Protestant work ethic is related to the spirit of capitalism, Catholicism, in Weber's view, did not hold any such implications. Indeed, there is an important strand of thought about work as such which makes Catholicism an important source of inspiration for organizers, wishing to break free from neoliberal mindset: the view that work is part of the human condition, a profoundly human activity, at best an expression of our humanity, at worst, punishment for the original sin. But it is not a way of redeeming oneself: abstaining from work does not have to be sinful, it can be a blessing reserved for those who follow a spiritual path, like Mary, who chose to contemplate Jesus' words, unlike the hard-working Martha. Idleness is a different matter, one should not live at the expense of others, if it can be avoided. Work is not an unconditional good. However, work is potentially world-building or person-expressing, a way of creating a better world.

What is critical is not work as such, but its intention and its expressive, symbolic function, as well as (obviously) that what is being done is not itself evil, malum in se. There is no virtue in being an industrious Mafioso or a punctilious commissar.[263]

Christianity (of all denominations) can bring the realization that love is an organizational virtue[264]. Love is the central tenet of Christian religion. It is inclusive and general, both normative and mystical, not earned but received by divine grace. The authors interviewed a group of Christian managers working for big and medium-sized corporations, as well as NGOs. They wished to find out how their interlocutors understood love in everyday work situations. It turns out that they described love as a virtue and they linked it to the sense of community. Organizational love can be seen as the building of virtue-oriented communities, transcending the role of productivity-seeking structures. It is one of the responsibilities of leadership to create the right conditions for the emergence of such love, but the foundation is spiritual and not just a matter of good management. The interviewees believed that *"organization is a human community of work"*[265] and people should come before profits, even though they tended to be in favour of regarding profitability as a key organizational goal. Love and respect should be directed to all people. The authors conclude that their:

> results suggest that managerial conceptions of love, while still being instrumental in orientation, can be a powerful antidote against individualism and narrow managerialist ideas about the role of organization. The development of the idea of the organization as community can be a lever to try and foster high-quality connections pervaded by love as an effective basis for neo-normative control[266].

Judaism can bring to organizations a sense of justice founded in traditional wisdom, recognizing the importance of rights and obligations of employers and employees at the workplace[267]. Justice is one of the central principles of Judaism and regarded as a cornerstone of society, including workplaces. Wealth is a responsibility, not legitimate if not approached with the principle of consideration and care for the less wealthy. The rights of employers are limited by this fundamental principle of justice. Both employees and employers are equal in the most basic respect of the human obligation before the divine. No setting can be seen as purely instrumental or economic, if there are human beings involved: they also have a social side, and as such cannot be lifted out of the moral context. The workplace is based on contractual relationships with two parties, where each has rights and obligations, yet one, the employees, have less of an advantage and thus should be given more attention and should be protected, especially if economically vulnerable. This is not purely an instrumental issue or matter of agreement, but a fundamental moral concern. Employers should pay wages on time. Employees should be able to work in safe conditions. Too great an income disparity is not legitimate. The employee should do decent work. These principles are not negotiable and they describe what is imperative for the social fabric. Judaism observes the moral necessity to be sensitive to the needs of others and thus invites trust as a characteristic of organizational relations. Judaism reminds us that workplaces cannot be seen as being located in a "moral vacuum".

Islam proposes a responsible approach to finance, which is increasingly appreciated, and not just in the Islamic parts of the world. Islamic banking[268] is based on the principle of profit and loss sharing, instead of the more conventional interest-based approach. Islamic law, the Shariah, prohibits paying or receiving interest, speculating and investing in industries such as alcohol and weapons. Banks are also expected to respect the pillars of Islam, especially almsgiving and the promotion of a productive use of money. Furthermore, Islam recommends employing a moral economy philosophy, including broader aims into the strategies of banks than purely financial gain. The leading idea is to support both economic and social welfare and to develop a fairer banking system. There exist more and less strictly religiously principled approaches to bank management[269], and the connection between invoked principles and practices is not equally strong for all banks. However, Islamic banks tend to be much more committed to vision and mission statements and they engage in a range of social activities. There is also a demonstrated connection between the dedication to CSR of these banks and their financial performance.

Buddhism may help to find a way of countering the prevalent tendency of contemporary organizations to be egocentric[270]. Buddhism challenges the self as illusory and proposes a spiritual practice which aims at a transformation of awareness, conquering the alienation of the mind from nature and society which leads to the self-centredness and egocentrism so prevalent in contemporary society. Meditation helps to break away from estrangement and to establish connection of everything with everything else and to foster a deep insight into the sense of the self. The result is "a nondual awareness that draws upon allocentric attentive processing (rather than egocentric) which is at home in groundlessness"[271]. Allocentric means focused on the other, rather than on the self. Organizations focused on the self become symptomatic of a collective sense of lack, driven by desires and motivations based on power and control, trying to escape anxiety, yet unable to cope with a collective sense of absence resulting from the inability to perceive and engage in the connectedness between everything. The isolation of the self as the one and true centre of agency erects rigid boundaries counteracting connectedness and co-operation. Furthermore, egocentric organizations tend to regard themselves as separated from the environment, including the natural environment. Such egocentricity is maladaptive, striving to protect against anxiety, but, instead, creating division and creating more fear as a reaction against imagined threat. It is an aggressive and arrogant management philosophy, enhancing destructive pursuits and unable to fulfil its promises, i.e. reduction of anxiety. It is based on a fantasy of omnipotence that institutionalizes greed and hostility. While Buddhist practice cannot change the economic system that generates this kind of structure, it certainly can show the practitioner that they are based on falsehood, and they may also help to understand that alternatives exist or can be found. Attempts to conceive of organizations as solid and separate will be met by failure, but Buddhism helps to see that this is a good thing. Egolessness bring hope of allocentric, non-dualistic ways of organizing. However, Buddhist mindfulness should not be used out of context, at the level of the individual, divorced from the religious system where it belongs – turned into a tool for the reproduction of corporate and institutional power it only serves to maintain toxic cultures[272]. Misappropriated as a technique minus the religion, it fails to make a difference and brings no revolution. Buddhist mindfulness has a soteriological purpose of cognitive liberation and enhancing moral and altruistic concern.

Zen Buddhism has an additional potential contribution to organizational practice and thinking through its tolerance and celebration of ambiguity in the form of koans[273]. Koans are highly ambivalent sayings, focusing on contradictions and paradoxes. The current tendency towards reductionism kills creativity and is completely incongruent with reality which abounds in dilemmas. Zen Buddhism may help to transcend this limited perspective through guidance on how to reconcile dilemmas by means of a form of cognition that transcends binary logic. The state of mind that develops with koan practice permits creative insight and thinking based on the logic of ambiguity. Zen Buddhism moves in the opposite direction of the Western quest for certainty and reductionist rationality.

Yet another important religious contribution to organizational liberation can be exemplified by the African philosophy and spirituality of Ubuntu, which can bring insights about possible new ways for building effective organizations[274]. According to Ubuntu, "A person is a person because of others,[275]" being human and being a person is always relational. People realize selfhood and humanity itself in the collective, by support, co-operation and mutualism. It cannot be achieved by rational thinking, but through heart and spirit and the embracing of spiritual practices based on the principles of discipline, morality, altruism, self and social consciousness, responsibility and duty. The social ideals that define Ubuntu practice are: solidarity, stewardship, dignity, compassion and care. While all of the principles can only be embraced by a perfect person, the Ubuntu spirituality encourages striving to do our best and believing in these ideas as guiding principles. Ubuntu goes directly against neoliberal doctrine and in itself is a strong proposition of an alternative approach for African organizations, to develop spiritual intelligence capable of conceiving of different, more humanistic, kinds of organizational roles and institutions. I believe that these lessons can well transcend the boundaries of the African continent.

Pope Francis, who is known as, at the same time, a religious leader and public intellectual holding quite radical ideas of social and economic change, speaks for hope seen as a religious feature, yet one that can and should be acted upon, not just individually, but socially. In my reading, it is also a plea for organization:

For us Christians, the future does have a name, and this name is Hope. Feeling hopeful does not mean to be optimistically naive and ignore the tragedy humanity is facing. Hope is the virtue of a heart that doesn't lock itself into darkness, that doesn't dwell on the past, does not simply get by in the present, but is able to see a tomorrow. Hope is the door that opens onto the future...A single individual is enough for hope to exist, and that individual can be you. And then there will be another "you", and another "you", and it turns into an "us". And so, does hope begin when we have an "us"? No. Hope began with one "you". When there is an "us", there begins a revolution[276].

The Pope regards this as a religious calling, but yet one that is to be practised in everyday life, in the world which we inhabit also outside of religious institutions, and outside of the structures of political or economic power. It is something we all can take part in and do something about.

The future of humankind isn't exclusively in the hands of politicians, of great leaders, of big companies [though] they do hold an enormous responsibility. But the future is, most of all, in the hands of those people who recognize the other as a "you" and themselves as part of an "us".[277]

4. See it rise!

Architecture
imagine an architecture / imagine a wall
by Reuben Woolley

they spread

> *deserts*

where they walk

> > *she saw*

it's no
> *slight*
> *coincidence. we*
complete a task

they say

we determine this sand
in

> > *straight*
> > *lines & arches*

we build
a city

& it's almost real[278]

Hopeful architecture
Marcus Vitruvius Pollo, better known as simply Vitruvius[279],

was an ancient Roman architect and engineer, considered to be one of the precursors of reflective architecture, who believed in the importance of three qualities of a construction: solidity, beauty and use. He also considered the organization of space as an important element of architecture. To him, unity was a matter of harmony. Parts should correspond with each other, and with the whole.

Beauty will be achieved when the appearance of a building is pleasing and elegant and the commensurability of its components is correctly related to the system of modules [measures][280].

To Vitruvius architecture was a profoundly interdisciplinary area, part of the knowledge about techniques as well as of the arts. To be a good architect, one has to be ready to engage in practice as well as in reflection. He considered immersion in activities ranging from drawing, via philosophy (of course) and music to physics, as crucial for the architect. Harmony is not just the desired quality of the structure, but also of the mind. Vitruvius was rediscovered during the Renaissance and his ideas were much celebrated, he inspired many artists and architects, including Leonardo da Vinci.

Another thinker with profound influence on how we conceive of architecture was the English art critic John Ruskin. The Seven Lamps of Architecture[281] consider architecture a political art, in the sense that it was a vital part of the human polity, even its embodiment. Not only the material side should be honoured, that is a mere building, but also the spiritual. The lamps are principles of good architecture, bringing to mind ideas of beauty, following the harmony of nature; truth, that is honesty, not hiding flaws behind the façade; sacrifice, or humility, a faith in a greater meaning; power, or shape and solidity; life, that is, vitality and dedication of the creators; memory, loyalty to the cultural context; and obedience to values. Good architecture unites people:

> How many and how bright would be the results in every direction of interest, not to the arts merely, but to national happiness and virtue, it would be as difficult to preconceive as it would seem extravagant to state: but the first, perhaps the least, of them would be an increased sense of fellowship among ourselves...[282]

The more contemporary (and still hugely controversial) architect Charles-Édouard Jeanneret, known as Le Corbusier[283,] shared the assumption that, while technology defines construction, architecture is defined by beauty. The architect "realizes as order which is a pure creation of his spirit...he determines the various movements of our heart and of our understanding; it is then that we experience the sense of beauty"[284]. This is not part of "anecdotal" art, but a source of meditation after a day's work, it is there for everyone. Architecture can bring us closer towards human welfare, making use of the revolutions in construction, making it possible to construct exact structures on a mass scale.

There is also a very practical and organizational aspect of architecture: the process of planning, designing and construction, that may involve a number of stakeholders, as it touches a variety of interests along the way. Peter Blundell Jones, Doina Petrescu and Kin Trogal[285] are among the proponents of the democratization of the process, advocating a more reflective approach and greater and broader involvement of different social actors, from researchers, designers and politicians to users and activists.

Architecture and organization

The beautiful book *Design Like You Give a Damn*[286] contains over 300 pages of examples of projects of simple and lovely inventions designed to help people in bad need of help with housing: earthquake victims, the homeless, war survivors; as well as structures to be used as community spaces, sanitation solutions and public policy projects. The collective author of the book was an organization creating and disseminating pro-bono projects around the world, providing transitional housing and other necessities, such as access to water. The founder Cameron Sinclair writes in the introduction that they wanted to demonstrate that "for every 'celebrity architect' there are hundreds of designers around the world, working under the ideal that it is not just how we build but what we build that truly matters"[287]. The book contains a large number of fascinating case studies, such as the paper church constructed in Kobe, Japan, 1995. As the name suggests, it is mainly made of lightweight materials: paper and polycarbonate, a cheap and exquisite structure, suffused with light and air. After the Great Hanshin earthquake, the parish became an important part of the community's disaster relief work and the temporary structure served as a base. It survived for 10 years before it gave way to a more permanent building. Another case is the Quinta Monroy Housing Project in Iquique, Chile dating from 2004, offering social housing to people who used to live in a slum area on the site, without displacing them. The architects explored informal settlements, learning about people's needs and preferences in order to propose a housing estate based on what they found out from the inhabitants and, at the same time, friendly, with an aura of spaciousness and light. The houses are shaped as cuboids, proportional but not the same, linked together in strings including single- and double-storey units. The plan assumes that the houses will grow, people will expand them, and it directs the expansion in a way that will make the habitation systematic, without overcrowding. Another stunning yet simple structure is presented in the case study of Rufisque Women's Centre in Senegal. Constructed between 1996 and 2001, it provides space for a large community centre for women. The architects first talked with the women who would be the future users of the structures, and made sure that the project would be useful and attractive for them. They used local material, with reuse and recycling, to create a space which looks quite impressive but is not costly or wasteful. The buildings are a warm shade of red, with supple lines and clean form, reminding me of the depictions of ancient Roman architecture with its stability and consciousness of light. The roofs bring shade and the spaces look cool but at the same time, light is welcome as an important part of the structures: it is let in by the material, such as "glass bricks" made of old bottles, wicker roofings, open colonaddes. The vast courtyards fulfil their traditional role as community centres, as the hearth where the women can feel at home and share their sense of belonging. There are many inexpensive and beautiful spaces for humans to use and inhabit presented in the book, but also some strikingly straightforward reactions to critical problems, such as paraSITE homeless shelter, designed in 1997 in New York. As the problem of homelessness continues to grow, also in rich countries such as the UK and US, much of the managed effort to "solve" it boils down to making public space uninhabitable and dangerous[288] by means of hostile architecture such as "homeless spikes" and sloping benches. A New York designer has proposed a simple counter tactic to one of these endeavours, the US city of Cambridge's introduction of "homeless-proof" vents, which were intended to prevent the homeless from sleeping on vents on the ground. The solution consists of an inflatable tent-like plastic tube, which can be attached to a public vent, and in which a person can sleep and remain warm. This is intended as a guerrilla type tactic but not as a solution to homelessness. By no means should homelessness be thought of as a "life style" or "individual choice", it should not be confirmed or accepted as part of modern society.

These are only a few examples taken from the book, I could go on for a long time trying to describe my joy at and admiration of the case stories and the photographs but I think I should, rather, recommend reading or leafing through the whole book. A much pleasurable experience and one which reminds me that we can make the world both more friendly to humans and less deadly to the planet we inhabit. But the question is, how can we make that happen around us, not just as an honourable exception? I think we do and to a significant extent we can do it by enlisting the help of architecture for everyday organizing.

Firstly, I think that architecture can bring sociality into organizing in a visible, embodied way. For example, two Polish British architects, Krzysztof Nawratek and Kasia Nawratek[289], consider the possibility of building a city open to diversity and difference. They propose the idea of radical inclusiveness, with roots in Christian tradition (but open to be embraced from many different perspectives, including Christian and non-Christian), dating back to Origen and his idea of Apocatastasis. They seek to promote an architecture which would help "to reconcile the freedom and autonomy of the individual with the idea of a collective political subject and the idea of community"[290]. Origen upheld that no one is rejected, and eventually, in a long and painful process, all creation will be redeemed and embraced by God. In more contemporary times, Teilhard de Chardin supported a similar belief in the Point Omega, or an evolution towards greater consciousness. While architecture cannot be conceived of as a point, it certainly can serve to attract consciousness and shared presence. The key feature of architecture is spatiality which, if taken very seriously, can help to exclude essentialism and linearity. An architect also has another important aspect in his or her toolbox, one corresponding with the Teilhardian idea of salvation for all as a process – and that is time. Architecture is also a process and can be encoded with multiple meanings that unravel or are co-created in time. The authors propose to consider architectural space using four perspectives: technical, or focused on the user; spatial, concentrated on geometry; temporal or process-oriented and linguistic, objects of communication. Architecture as radical inclusion is not a pragmatic programme, but a goal, an idea towards the process slowly develops, a:

> revolutionary change aiming to free the architecture from the clutches of the neoliberal paradigm and the logic of short term profit. It could free architecture from being a mere by-effect of land speculation[291].

Perhaps not by itself capable of bringing about political and social change, architecture nevertheless is a powerful and meaningful act of materialization of the social, a statement both visible and endurable. Citizenship can be made to mean not privilege but belonging, realized by inclusion into the system of the city[292]. Architecture is a language of the law that makes it possible to realize and encourage a communication process leading towards greater inclusion and participation, a way of taking responsibility for the envisioning of a future. It is important to be able to open the future rather than close it down (as neoliberal urbanist programmes tend to do by means of exclusion, privatization and giving up of meaning to big data). It does not mean giving up of vision and aim, quite the contrary: it is necessary to know what kind of future we want and what consequences architectural choices are having. But what we need is an ethical foundation rather than a materialistic one.

Secondly, architecture can make a big contribution towards greater resilience of organizations. Constantin Petcou and Doina Petrescu[293] present a framework for resilient urban regeneration and demonstrate the importance of active engagement of key stakeholders in the architectural process. Austerity and environmental damage prompt solutions that would make urban communities, seen as complex systems embedded in an ecological context, resilient and democratic. Cities need to be able to adapt to changing conditions and develop a self-governing agency. Based on a case study of a French suburban town, Colombes, the authors present strategies for such a programme, including recycling and eco-construction projects, co-operative housing, and urban agriculture units. Their architecture stages the issues they tackle, such as recycling and local production, by means of buildings and design. It also provides tools and spaces for the manifestation of resilient practices, and co-produces a new infrastructure which is a new form of commons:

> it organises a range of spatial, temporal and human interstices and transforms them into shared facilities, it sets up a different type of urban space, neither public nor private, to host reinvented collective practices and collaborative organisations, it initiates networks of interstices to reinvent commons in metropolitan contexts. This type of organisation involves forms of commoning, ways of ensuring the expansion and sustainability of the shared pool of resources, but also ways of commonality as a social practice[294].

Thirdly, architecture can make a statement that transcends the role of the static slogan and is able to mobilize and even serve as a means of the emancipatory change process. Organization theorist Tuomo Peltonen[295] proposes that the study of architecture and space may significantly alter, even revolutionize, organization research. It brings in a number of perspectives that had been previously marginalized or left out. It may help us to understand how particular social-material collectives emerge and invite a more heterodox view of organizing itself. In his intensely engaging book *Holes in the Whole*, architect and social scientist Krzysztof Nawratek[296] presents a vision of architecture that places it at the forefront of radically hopeful organizing. He advocates true urban change, not brought about by the acquiring of power, but through "understanding the mechanisms, which will allow restoration of the city's subjectivity and will regain the power to

shape the city's own destiny and future"[297]. In Nawratek's idea
of the city it is not about a "build-up area" or an assemblage of
buildings and infrastructure, but a context for sociality, space
for human co-existence in relationships and interactions. Cities
can offer a context not just for "being" but for "becoming":
emancipative change, innovation, creation. Architecture can
provide a language and a symbolism that makes it more likely
to happen, and it also can set out borders that are sufficiently
actively permeable to be able to mediate contact with the outside
world, without making the community vulnerable to rampant
neoliberal globalization. Cities can keep a certain collective
agency that is necessary to renounce the much harmful passivity
in the face of the predatory workings of contemporary capital.
It is far from a given and it needs to be actively reclaimed and
maintained – and here is the place for what I see as a large role to
be played by conscious effort undertaken by many organizations
from different sectors. Nawratek invites such an interpretation:

> It is time we came back to the discussion about democracy.
> I do believe in the power of the people. I do believe that
> the essence of the city is that it self-manages and that the
> community not only inhabiting it but also using it should
> govern itself. But this community is much more than just a set
> labelled "people". It is much more complex because of games
> and interdependencies between power and knowledge…[298]

This is where organization theory and practice and architecture
can work together for something of a revolutionary programme,
something which the book by itself refrains from providing.

Architecture is a potent ally but can also serve as a harsh
antagonist. It has demonstrably influenced the way we use
space, the way we conceive of it and how we imagine its role
and function. It has also determined the way we think of cities,
organizations and of management itself[299]. Friendly architecture

can help us organize better – and it certainly helps us to dream bolder and better.

I asked Krzysztof Nawratek for a comment, a short personal manifesto for architecture and he said the following:

I believe architecture has a paradoxical inclusive potential – it could help people to act together keeping them separated. Multi-storey building is not only a way to increase financial output from the single plot of land, but it is also a way to resolve a tension between many economic actors competing over this piece of space. The wall dividing a room allows multiplicity of activities to happen simultaneously. Architecture operates between abstract, spatial relationships and very concrete programmes and meanings associated with spaces and materiality. Architecture works in sync with hegemonic political and economic regimes, but is able to create small, temporary autonomous spaces and liberation and emancipation.

I happen to live in one such dream embodied in hopeful architecture. Park Hill flats in Sheffield was a brutalist housing estate designed by Jack Lynn and Ivor Smith under the supervision of John Lewis Womersely and constructed in the early 1960s. The aim was to provide affordable and comfortable housing to inhabitants of slums and substandard back-to-back accommodation from the area. The architecture was at the same time imaginative and simple, as well as functional, offering all modern comforts. The inhabitants moved in street by street, as they used to live in the old neighbourhoods, not losing touch with their communities. The floors of the buildings were called after the old streets, which earned the estate the poetic name *Streets in the Sky*[300]. During the 60s the estate was popular in the media and well loved by the inhabitants, a dramatic improvement in living standards and conditions. The next decade was marked by the beginning of economic problems and the flats ceased to be as affordable as intended. The next decade brought about a drastic deterioration in the housing situation throughout the UK, which seriously affected Park Hill. The buildings were not properly maintained, housing policies made it impossible to continue cultivating the old social spirit and from a utopian "community within a community" the estate took a quick and sad tumble towards urban slum. On a Facebook forum dedicated to brutalism, one of the discussants remembers these days as bleak and difficult:

> Ben Freeman: I was a student when I lived in Park Hill, with drug dealers on one side of me and a brothel the other side. I would have loved to live with students but I couldn't afford even the cheapest student housing, the only place I could afford was Park Hill...[301]

I have been in touch with some more permanent former Park Hill inhabitants from these times and their stories are similar: of decay, neglect, increasing violence and poverty, but also of anger at the authorities who seemed to have ceased caring. There was a feeling that the same fate would befall this estate as so many others: that is that it would be closed down and demolished. However, unexpectedly to some but not to those with an interest for architecture, the building was Grade II* listed in 1998. It stood for many years uninhabited until a recent (2009) re-development project undertaken by a private developer, Urban Splash, together with English Heritage, aiming to turn the flats into apartments, business units and social housing. The renovation takes place in phases and two large parts of the building have already been refurbished more or less according to plan, except that not many of the promised cafes, social spaces, shops or pubs have materialized. But the place still hosts dreams, as strong as it once did. In a fairly recent BBC programme about the estate[302] both old and new residents expressed their hopes connected to Park Hill. One of the inhabitants says this is much more than just a residential area, he believes that it is "my home, and these are my neighbours"[303]. He says that it was:

> set up with such high ideas trying to make a place for people where they could live together using architecture to create a community. In the end it did not work so well but we feel we're doing it again. And it's a lovely feeling.[304]

Many of my neighbours, and myself, have expressed similar feelings. Park Hill is beautiful and it stands for a beautiful idea which has attracted us to the place as much as its visual charm. It inspires artists such as, perhaps most famously, Mandy Payne[305] who has dedicated much of her work to the estate, including a series of pictures created on pieces of concrete in celebration of brutalist architecture. Films are being made, such as Park Hill re-imagined[306], featuring several of the inhabitants, who are narrating Park Hill as an aesthetic and social experience. Books such as Park Hill Sheffield in black and white[307] present the estate in a broader context of architecture and sociological vision. There is an idea among architects, especially typical for modernism, to see architecture as redemption through order, beauty and function. It is an impossible idea but it keeps returning. Perhaps it should not be cast away but approached more "modestly and politically, making small moves toward a reinvented world"[308]. This calls for:

> a move away from the strictures of order, so that architecture, far from being a straightjacket for social control, becomes a crucible for social exchange, in which contingency is not seen as a derided threat but as an opportunity[309].

The current renovation by architects of Urban Splash is rooted in the same dreams and ideas. The old architecture has been treated with respect and care, and the modernization is both functional and imaginative. But as the project proceeds, some issues are dropped, and new ones arise. There is still an uninhabited, decaying part waiting for reconstruction. At the moment of writing this, the intended social housing programme, has been limited and replaced by a project to invest in the development of upmarket student accommodation. Another participant of the brutalist Facebook forum is greeting the decision with mixed feelings:

> Simon Fairhead: It should all be social housing. There is such a shortfall right now, we shouldn't really be building anything else. Let the students find digs in dodgy Victorian terraces like we used to. I had running water in my student room. It was running down the wall, mind you...[310]

Student accommodation seems to be the main feature of new constructions in the area.

> Joe Ondrak: I'm not fussed about it becoming student accommodation since nearly every new building project in Sheffield is student accommodation right now. There are two universities in the (relatively small) city, and since the cap has been lifted on student intake numbers, the population of undergrads has exploded – so in that respect, it's a predictable and logical move.

He further explains:

> Joe Ondrak: I live 2 minutes away from this and right now, doing *anything* with the unused blocks is a welcome change. As of last year, Urban Splash erected a 7ft security fence (covered in anti-climb paint) around the entire grounds

of Park Hill, booting out the community of homeless people who found shelter in its grounds, and preventing maintenance to the grounds to be carried out. It's gone from looking somewhat neglected, but still interesting landmark with mowed and trimmed grounds, to an utterly overgrown and depressing space in about a year[311].

Since I arrived in the UK in the mid-nougthies, the problem with homelessness has been gaining in urgency and magnitude. As I write this, the entire city of Sheffield, like most other UK cities and towns, is full of homeless people of all ages, begging by shop entrances and ATMs, every day, come rain or shine. Some time ago, a small tent city was set up at Park Hill, self-managed by the homeless people living in the area. They revealed that there have been people living in the old dilapidated part of the estate and they declared that they volunteered to help clean up the area with the hope of acquiring a place to live once the old part gets renovated. The reactions from the council and the developer were negative and soon the tent settlement was cleared away. At the time of writing this, there is an intensive clearance going on in the area. In addition to the closing off of the old part of the estate, bushes and green areas around are cut down and replaced with lawns, all in the hope of keeping the homeless away. Some of the residents are not happy with the development.

Joe Ondrak: The utter ignorance of Sheffield's growing homeless community and affordable social housing in the renovation of Park Hill has utterly soured my association with the place, which is a shame because I used to love walking through the grounds and taking it in. The huge billboard up past the amphitheater behind the station has the audacity to proudly claim "apartments from £100,000". As nice as it is that the building is being used, the management have been doing so in a complete antithesis to the spirit of its original construction.

The dream seems, once again, to be giving way to a harsher, bleaker reality. But it does not disappear, as long as the building keeps towering over the landscape of Sheffield city. It reminds us daily of what we could be, of what a city can mean for its inhabitants. A symbol and material proof for that solidarity and hope are still important for us, even though we may not know how to live them.

Radical politics
A politics of hope

Radical politics is a way of collective thinking and acting which aims to change social structures and institutions in a fundamental way, together with cultural values and leading ideas. It can refer to change from the perspective of the right or left. In this book I will focus on the left, as I believe that it is this side of the political spectrum that can bring hope for a fairer, more equal and more democratic society, including more democratic organizations. It can concern international or local matters, pertain to social issues and/or the natural environment. The corner stone in radical politics is a conviction that history is not predetermined, socio-political systems are not given by God or laws of nature and humans can influence their collective destiny.

One of the most well-known figureheads of radical politics is the Genevan and French Enlightenment philosopher Jean-Jacques Rousseau. His ground-breaking mid-eighteenth century treatise *Discourse on Inequality*[312] is one of the most powerful critiques of civilization ever written. He considers private property as the source of inequality and proposes that human nature, in its original state, does not justify unfairness. According to Rousseau there exist two natural principles of human nature: self-preservation and pity, or empathy. Both are instinctive and based on sentience, and from them spring the "natural needs" human beings share. It is civilization and reason that create all other needs, and it is first at this stage that inequality takes root. People became settled and claimed land and other possessions. Then the division of labour was introduced and caused further divisions. Rousseau's ideas were much celebrated by Enlightenment thinkers and reformers, including the Jacobins and the founders of the USA.

The second key figure I would like to present in this section is Karl Marx, whom I have already briefly introduced. Karl Marx was a philosophical giant, whose thought dating from the nineteenth century still stands valid to a large extent. He has famously proclaimed that while "[t]he philosophers have only interpreted the world, in various ways, [now] the point is to change it"[313]. His analysis and critique of the capitalist economic system in four volumes, *Das Kapital,* continues to have momentous influence on theorists and activists alike. The most widely cited of the four, volume one[314], concerns the contradictions hidden within the capitalist mode of production. The analysis shows how capital has come into being by the division of people into owners and workers and continuing through expropriation. It forms a basis for a radical programme of redressing the balance by means of radical social change towards socialism.

American linguist Noam Chomsky is a contemporary thinker, inspiring radical politics for social and economic equality. He is a very prolific author, both as linguist and as anarcho-socialist political philosopher. Of many well-known books, *Occupy*[315] is a good example of his ideas and practical engagement for social change. In 2011 during the Occupy movement's spread across various countries, he became its vocal and very articulate supporter. The book presents a critique of the capitalist system and provides an explanation of the movement's aims and propositions of reform: rejection of austerity, greater democratization, abandonment of self-centredness as the main economic and political principle and a de-imperialization of US foreign policy. He proposes direct participative democracy as better suited to contemporary society than the traditional representative order.

Radical politics of organization

Nigel Slack[316] is one of the Occupy movement participants who did not give up engagement in active politics, albeit not on the national, but local level. He is well known locally for his commitment to finding out how decisions are made at Sheffield City Council, the workings of power, and his dedication to the mission of making the citizens better represented in the decision-making bodies. He often calls for increased citizen participation in local politics in local media and on his blog. I asked him to share his reflections on the importance of such engagement and what follows is his response to my request.

Nigel Slack: Why is it important to be a local activist?

The importance of local political activism, whether small or large scale, cannot be overestimated. It may seem something of a generalization but local politicians, just like their national counterparts, and the public servants that support them, would rather make decisions based on their own agendas and their "ideals" about what is best for the locality and its people. This applies as much at regional (or sub-national) level as it does locally and yet decisions at these levels can have more impact than those made nationally.

As an "Active Citizen", someone who is deeply involved in and cares for my locality, my city in this case, I try to encourage local institutions to make the best decisions possible and to mitigate the potentially bad decisions that are about to be made. In trying to achieve this I live by a couple of basic tenets: firstly, the public should know all we can about the business of the decision-makers that affect our lives, our wallets and our democracy. Secondly, to try and improve the levels of transparency and accountability within City Council and other institutions. And thirdly, to shine a light on how decisions are made and where the money goes. This approach can help us all to understand the business of running a city and enable us to ensure the benefit of decisions is in favour of the citizens first and foremost. Importantly, we must all remember that, whether we are involved in our local politics or not, the decisions made on our behalf by politicians and public servants will have deep and long-term impacts on the fabric, services, environment and, most importantly, people of our city.

Citizens of all kinds, residents, workers, business owners, students, rich and poor alike, deserve a say in how our localities are run. Beyond an occasional visit to a ballot box we can and should be aware of what our local decision-makers are doing to us and we should be able to have our say, supported by transparent and accountable information, on the choices before us.

How local democracy works, how decisions are made, how they are influenced and how, as a citizen to get involved, should be part of what we learn before we are of an age to even cast a vote. In particular those who are often portrayed as "future leaders", be that in politics, business or community, should be keenly aware of the way local decisions are made and understand the impact on future citizens of decisions made now. Only then can we hope that individual or collective local campaigns, by informed "Active Citizens", can effectively safeguard what we treasure about where we live.

Radical organizing

Radical organizing makes it possible to engage in active and sustainable resistance to neoliberal colonization of the economy. Maria Daskalaki and George Kokkinidis[317] depict how self-managed organizations, such as Greek Vio.me, create spaces of solidarity and how these spread throughout the social fabric through meetings and resistance laboratories, where people share ideas and experiences and create social events such as concerts. The studied organizations were able to produce needed symbolic and material resources by making use of their embeddedness in the space they inhabit by an interplay of fixity and mobility. They use extensively their local ties as well as moving to establish connections with other organizations to mobilize the resources they need. They "establish bridges across spatial scales in order to consolidate and diffuse resources, experiences and knowledge for the co-production of new forms of resistance and post-capitalist alternatives"[318]. Co-operatives demand extra members or resources from the solidarity initiatives which mobilize the needed support. In such ways, the organizations connect the local and the translocal through solidarity events and members' mobility schemes. The organizing processes that develop are able to successfully challenge the dominant neoliberal order. Eloise Helena Livramento Dellangelo, Steffen Böhm and Patrícia Maria Emerenciano de Mendonça[319] propose further insights from radical politics of resistance for organizational settings by adopting three key political discourse theory concepts: dislocation, identity and chains of equivalence. Dislocation is the naming of events and ideas that cannot find representation within the dominating context and thus disturb it. Identity helps to build cohesion among participants in a counter-hegemonic movement. Chains of equivalence signify creating equivalent identities that negate the dominant system. The authors portray some recent processes of organizing resistance, such as the slow food movement and resisting airport extensions in the UK, showing how these instances successfully use these political strategies. They do this by mobilizing such organizational roles and processes as leadership, communication and decision-making in ways that culminate in the political strategies. The authors conclude that politics and organizing can directly contribute reciprocally to each other in order to support social movements that resist oppression and injustice.

Radical politics is also able to bring forward realistic organizational alternatives, based on self-management, both resulting in the emergence of new organizational forms and in societal change. For example, Thomas Swann and Konstantin Stoborod[320] propose that anarchism can have a constructive contribution to a number of key organizational issues, supporting autonomy and anti-authoritarian leadership. Perhaps most importantly, it can "reawaken a suppressed and yet vital capacity for critical imagination"[321], allowing for asking questions of the very notion of organization and breaking through assumptions deeply embedded in capitalist ideology and so reclaiming new territories for thinking and praxis.

Radical ethics inspired by Emmanuel Lévinas' concept of an-archy, or of dropping the categorizations of people and unconditional opening up to the Other, can inform the way business ethics is rethought and reclaimed as a moral guideline for organizing and management, recommends Carl Rhodes[322]. What is usually called "business ethics" in textbooks and business jargon does not have a status of its own, but is at best subordinated to financial and market dictated goals. That kind of "ethics" is indeed a justification for amoral or immoral activities. Introducing a strong and radically moral voice turns the tables: ethics does not have another purpose than creating a sense of responsibility for the Other. Dissent as a moral engagement is justified to defend our humanity against corporate excesses. Such an attitude is instrumental in the pursuing of radical democracy and resisting the close to absolute sovereignty of business in today's societies and the claim of corporate immutability as an inherent systemic issue. An-archy is an engagement with the Other without the mediation of principle, in ways that cannot be fully controlled or grasped by rationality. Lévinasian ethics disturbs any justification of subjugation of the Other to external goals, such as profit maximization. It identifies "a self that is not the same as that which is conceived of consciously and represented in discourse; a singular identity that defies thematization"[323]. We are responsible to and for the Other before we enter any other engagement with the world or ourselves. Economy is a necessary relationship and work, which undoes the self, is one of its central themes, but through ethical anarchy the authority of this theme is decentred and replaced by the unconditional authority of alterity, thus supporting ethically based justice. Understood this way, "business ethics" is not the task of business but of society as a whole. We all need to be morally involved with the dealings of corporations to regain the agency that has been unjustly taken away from us, under the guise of effective management or economic growth. And this agency can be used for taking control. Anarchism and radical politics promote self-management and self-determination and may help to re-configure them to fit contemporary organizational settings. Marcelo Vieta[324] proposes that the tradition of self-management, derived to a great degree from anarchism and radical politics, has not lost its relevance today and has an important continuance in the co-operativist movement in the twenty-first century. The idea at the heart of the tradition as well as the new movement is that it is possible and desirable to free oneself from the exploitative capitalist mode of production through taking active responsibility for organization and management in ways that, on the one hand, can be traced back to modes of production and exchange based on reciprocity, and, on the other, in political organized action. Alternative modes of management and organization are being interlaced with the values and ethics of the desired world, "creating the new inside of the shell of the old"[325]. The new system is foreshadowed in the residue of the old and so the economic self-determined activities are at the same time the taking of a radical political position and actively pursuing it. Vieta emphasizes that self-management simultaneously frees the workers from capitalist oppression and prefigures a future, more just system. It is a way of moving beyond capitalism while still encapsulated within its "irresistible" institutions, presented as having "no alternative". He names the three main principles of self-management:

(1) the *effectiveness* and *viability* of associated forms of social production for provisioning for life's needs and producing social wealth; (2) economic justice in some form of *democratic organization* of productive entities; and (3) the *social ownership* of the means of production.[326]

By adopting these principles, we are gradually building not just a better management system, but a better society from below and to a large extent under the neoliberal radar, as none of these principles even exist in the managerialist imaginarium, "in spite of the system, as pockets of possibility within planetary capital, increasingly offering a more compelling model for people to secure their economic and social needs and desires"[327]. However, as I point out in my book *Occupy Management!*[328], the organizers are able to freely use, reuse and recycle a large number of managerial ideas and models for their own purposes and on their own terms, while radically rejecting neoliberal ideologies and rationalities.

British and Greek organization theorist and academic activist Maria Daskalaki believes that self-management inspired by radical politics has the potential to make a real difference in today's world:

Self-management is a fight for equality, solidarity, direct democracy and social justice. I am researching self-management because I want the world to change, become a better place. Over the last few years my country has become another victim of aggressive neoliberal capitalism and people are becoming poorer and poorer every day. Young people with HE will never find jobs, will never be able to live with dignity. People have reacted though what is taking place is far from a revolution. It is a slow realization however that we need to change the way we organize our working life; self-organize our work, get rid of managers and repressive structures who strip our work from emotion, affect and pathos. Self-management for me is a reason to be an academic and write – write about great stories of genuine struggle and resistance. It reminds me that there is a reason to believe in utopia because this belief keeps you alive and gives you tools to continue against all odds. While studying self-management, I get to meet great people; people who are looking the capitalist beast straight in the eyes and say 'no, there is an alternative'![329]

I remember Solidarność of August 1980 and the year that followed in Poland. I was living in Sweden then and when the strike in the Gdańsk Shipyard began, I was about to start my studies at Lund University. The TV set attracted me more than it ever had. I watched the news whenever I could. All I could think of was actually getting there. And so, finally, I did. It was late October when I stepped out of the train at Warsaw Central Railway Station. I did not want to waste any time, so, despite being penniless, I jumped into a taxi and told the driver I wanted to go to 5, Szpitalna street. "Lady, to that address I'm gonna drive you for free. You are my guest," he said. I felt like the car had risen up into the air. Everything was absolutely easy, even though it was, at the same time, palpably impossible. We were walking on water, just like that, and we knew we did. I thanked the cab driver wholeheartedly and he laughed. I ran up the stairs and, panting, opened the door. The headquarters of the Masovia region of the Solidarność trade union. "I want to become a member." In the end, I did not: I was not working or even studying in Poland. But the kind woman took down my name as a sympathizer and I got a badge with Solidarność on it. The whole week was like that. Clear, intense, impossible. The long evenings at my grandparents' place: my grandfather was a worker and his friends and neighbours used to come over to talk politics and smoke a lot of cigarettes. The air was thick like dusk. They knew they were living in a time that was both absolutely real and perfectly out of the question. People I met in the streets were smiling at each other, at me. Bus drivers whistled, shop assistants looked like they were stopping themselves from dancing almost with the utmost self-control. I realized I most certainly was Polish, after all. I realized the whole world was Polish, whether it knew it, or not. I came back several times in 1980 and 1981, and things got more difficult, there was a looming sense of danger, the country was ravaged by strikes and political tension. Yet there was a sense of calm purpose among the people I knew.

Some days ago, I found myself standing in Mokotowska street together with David Ost, the sociologist famous for his almost prophetic writings about Solidarność and democracy in Poland[330]. He pointed to one of the buildings and told me how, on the night of 13 December 1981, he ran over to this place, the then location of Solidarność headquarters, to check if things were alright, and was told neither the military nor the police were there (but had been before and would be back). The Martial Law of December 1981 was proclaimed, the dancing days were over. Solidarność was banned, its leaders and activists jailed, a curfew imposed and the borders sealed. I was in Sweden then and intending to visit Poland for Christmas, but I was not allowed to board the ferry, just like the rest of the passengers. It was all over. Everything took a different turn. But the days remained in my bones. I still carry them around with me wherever I go. I have been there, talked with the people, inhaled the air thick with smoke, walked the streets of Warsaw. I know this is real, even though it could not happen; I know it is still there, under the pavements, in the bones of people like me, under the surface of drab common sense. Even under the surface of austerity.

Because it is bound to spring up sometimes: humanity is not quite linear, and sometimes it is compelled to stray onto the road of solidarity, instead of continuing walking on straight ahead.

Alternative organizations
Simply, organizations

Alternative organizations are simply the rich organizational ecosystem that exists outside of mainstream management textbooks. Organization theorist Martin Parker made the term popular in his calls for taking into consideration something outside the very limited scope of interest that business schools seem to be focusing on:

> Let's think about it in a different way. Can you imagine studying in a biology department which only teaches animals with four legs and omits the rest? Or getting a degree in history based on studying a part of 17th-century Staffordshire? This is what business schools are doing[331].

He goes on to listing organizations such as the Mafia, the Amish and the Zapatistas as also belonging to the area of study.

Indeed, organizations outside of the standard business textbook example have been the object of study and theorizing for a long time, at least as long as organization and management studies existed as a discipline. One of the most well-known classical inquires, conducted within a more traditional corporate setting, was dedicated to alternative organizing. While conducting a series of experiments in the Western Electric plant in Hawthorne (Cicero), 1927-1932, Elton Mayo[332] observed informal processes of organizing that awoke his interest. Within a well-designed organizational structure, there were informal groups and leaders with little or no connection to the formal system. Social integration turned out to be a major motivator and a factor driving people to self-organize: people have a need to co-operate and communicate. It is group standards that, to a large extent, determine individual actions and people are more willing to conform to spontaneous group norms than to formal ones, which they may perceive as limiting or alien. Social needs are just as important in the workplace as economic ones and feelings are part of the organizing process.

Another seminal study of organizations we today would call alternative is William Foote Whyte's[333] investigation of organizations in a poor Italian district of Boston, referred to by the author as Cornerville during the years of the Great Depression of the 1930s. He observed both formal organizations, such as the Italian Association in Cornerville, as well as informal ones, such as street gangs. These organizations provided a social setting for people for how they worked and acted together, but also how they fought, flirted, gambled and imagined a future for themselves. Social communities are a powerful way of connecting in a more purposeful way, while not sacrificing people's fundamental social needs to aims such as effectiveness or productivity. Whyte opened his readers' eyes to this vital issue, and to the fact that the informal organizations he studied navigated within a set of norms and rules of their own home community. They were perceived as legitimate within the setting, even if the wider populace regarded them as borderline criminal. Furthermore, they gave people a sense of agency that otherwise would not have been within their reach. They were able to achieve more than if they had been acting individually, both in terms of economy and politics.

Another fundamental example of alternative organizations is presented in Erving Goffman's[334] 1960s influential study of total organizations aspiring to having total control of their members. They separate their participants from the environment with physical barriers such as fences, security services, strict regulations, and become places:

of residence and work where a large number of like-situated

individuals, cut off from the wider society for an appreciable period of time, together lead an enclosed, formally administered round of life.[335]

Some examples of organizations of this kind are: prisons, concentration camps, battleships, hospitals, boarding schools and mental clinics, one of which was Goffman's study object. The clinic aspired to control and change one of the groups of participants: the patients. Other participants, doctors, nurses, and cleaning personnel, were following a different and less totalizing order. One of the main control strategies adopted was the complete abolition of the patients' privacy. There was no possibility for them to construct and sustain an identity because, unlike in civil society, they were not surrounded by people that support, or at least respect, such attempts. Their identity was defined in advance, without them being present and sometimes also against their will. This is an effective control strategy but one which excludes any genuine social engagement and participation. Goffman upholds that total organizations produce socially disabled persons. However, the study also shows how many people did not passively submit to these practices, and were able to save their own dignity and individuality, by informal and underground organizing. Patients were meeting clandestinely to smoke, which had a powerful meaning, transcending the purely recreational: they were distancing themselves from roles that were imposed on them and confirming a social identity of their own. They were symbolically expressing the ability to maintain moderate control over time and space, as well as over their body, but perhaps most significantly, they were collectively taking responsibility for the prohibited act.

Without something to belong to, we have no stable self, and yet total commitment and attachment to any solid unit implies a kind of selflessness. Our sense of being a person can come from being drawn into a wider social unit; our sense of selfhood can arise through the little ways in which we resist the pull. Our status is backed by the solid buildings of the world, while our sense of personal identity often resides in the cracks[336].

Goffman's famous dictum, "whenever worlds are laid on, underlives develop"[337,] can be regarded as a motto for many contemporary researchers interested in alternative organizing.

There is an (organizational) alternative

Several years ago, depressed by the increasingly streamlined and bleak picture of management and organizing I was seeing all around me, I had a coffee and a chat with a good old friend, Polish activist and alternative organizer. I shared my thoughts with her on how the organizational world seemed to become more are more limited, closed and impossible for me to feel at home in. She said: "Oh, but there *is* an alternative!"

I said: "Yes, I know, Greenpeace, but I mean, economic organizations, they are all the same now."

She shook her head: "No, no, that's what I mean, you should study them, email this person, she will tell you some interesting things."

So I emailed Gosia of the Green Hostel[338] and she did talk to me (when I mentioned my activist friend), and she did, indeed, tell me some interesting things. It turned out that they were a group of radical people, tired of the conventional work organizations, who wished to create a workplace for themselves where they would feel at home – and they wanted to share the feeling with others and that's how they came up with the idea of starting a hostel in Warsaw city centre. They had no hierarchy; everything was done by democratic process. They had no formal rules, but strong ethnical principles which had to be accepted by all the organizers. Everything took a long time to decide but they were doing well economically and seemed happy enough, even if there was no lack of conflict. This looked very interesting indeed. I kept returning for interviews and observations and asked for recommendations about whom else to contact and study. The snowball effect caught on, I was introduced to new organizations and people, usually referring to my friend the activist, who is respected and well-liked by most of the people in my field, who are otherwise quite unwilling to let outsiders in, be it politicians, journalists or researchers (especially senior ones, like myself). I came in contact with collectives and groups of people running vegan restaurants, a kindergarten, an independent magazine, an arts and technology community centre, co-operative shops, and many others. My investigations extended from Poland to the UK, thanks to an EU grant that I acquired and I spent much time on intensive field research, using ethnographic methods, such as interview, observation, later on also participant observation. This research is still ongoing, even though less intensively, as I have also other duties. Some of the organizations are growing, most are doing well economically or at least making do, even in austerity-driven UK. They are all dedicated to a set of principles, such as veganism or co-operativism, and work is valued as a human need. Some apply direct democracy, while others use other, more structural democratic methods, such as committees, posts with limited terms, rotation. In important matters they rely on meetings and collective decision-making. Many of my interviewees expressed a conviction that they were working outside of the capitalist system or at its margins and saw themselves as an alternative to that system, one, which, hopefully, one day may be able to grow into a new and better system, based on economic justice and where meaningful work will be a human right. I keep writing about my research experiences, but if I were to recommend just one publication, I'd choose an early stage book, *Occupy Management!*[339], where I outline the main ideas and principles of such an alternative management programme.

Adam Makuszewski is one of my interviewees and one of Poland's imaginative young co-operative and green activists. I asked him why it was so important to engage in grass-root alternative organizing. He pointed to the unpredictability of the contemporary world. Everything seems to be in crisis: the welfare state, neoliberal economy, migration and climate change. For Adam self-organization is a way of trying to regain control over the things in the world most important to us, which we do not want to lose. It is an emotional response, one involving a symbolic relationship which defines who we are. Some people feel a calling to take responsibility for the world around them. A good example of such an attitude are the environmental activists defending the Białowieża Forest, an ancient natural preserve, from being destroyed by an aggressive logging campaign launched by the Polish government in 2017[340]. It is important because biodiversity is of great value in itself, but also because people feel responsible for the forest and its natural wild state. Furthermore, the market generates prices which are much higher than what many people want to pay. Self-organization can help with that too, because it can dramatically reduce waste (and become even more ecologically sound in the process). Adam presents the consumers' co-operative "Dobrze" as an example of the successful engagement by local communities, bringing advantages to themselves, by being able to provide cheap and healthy food, to the farmers producing food which is sold at the co-op's shops, which offer them much better conditions than the supermarkets, and to the natural environment, because the production is sustainable and ecological. But that is not all: equally important are the democratic values, such as open membership, co-operative principles, economic participation and self-education. People organize around these values and do not have to be "motivated" externally – these values are, in fact, their motivation. The aim for self-organization is also something that exists in the community, around which people come together. Adam says that parents organize to help children to safely get to school, pensioners come together to keep an eye on the neighbourhood, and these are typical bottom-up examples. But there also exist good examples of support from the authorities and bigger organizations, such as on Borneo, where members of local communities can get access to cheaper healthcare if they refrain from cutting trees in the equatorial forests. Self-organization can enhance resilience and help to achieve sustainability. Someone needs to promote self-organizations, there is a need for activists, Adam believes, who are able to mobilize others, show that it is worthwhile engaging in this kind of activity which lies outside of the mainstream of the economic and political system. Their role is not to manage but to mediate between knowledge, values, trust, local identities and resources, and they need to believe and have hope in a better world.

The most important truth revealed by the study of alternative organizations is that there is, in fact, an alternative. Martin Parker's *Alternative Business*[341] offers examples of fictional and historical narratives of organizations outside of the current limited mainstream, from pirates to the Mafia, presented as able to offer valid insights and ideas for organizing today. He explicitly proposes that these cases can challenge the assumption of no alternative and demonstrates how they can help us to understand better how organizing and culture are interlinked and support each other. For example, the legend of Robin Hood presented in one of the first chapters, uniting many of the traits and ideas presented throughout the book, represents the trickster archetype and an important theme in outlaw narratives: the romantic character of noble bandit and defender of justice and the poor. It is an interesting heroic story made up of contradictions, both fact and fiction, presenting a protagonist loyal to the king but also a rebel, part of old and contemporary culture, and placed in an ambiguous boundary area between law and crime. He both organizes and disorganizes the understanding of collective effort and he clearly represents economic order, albeit it is not easy to define which and how it should be judged. Robin shapes the iconic principles of organizational counter culture: the dream and ideal of just revenge against inequality and oppression. He functions as a label for many outlaw stories – there are probably many Robin Hoods. The moral of these tales can be about the bringing to attention of radical alternatives and the questioning of the legitimacy of hegemonic power, whatever it may be at the time. But as a pop-culture character Robin does not necessarily have radical politics:

> Just like any argument about culture more generally, it is difficult to distinguish between a mass culture that numbs and a counter culture that offers alternatives. Robin seems to be both[342].

A similar case can be made for the other characters presented in the book, such as pirate and robber tales, cowboys, Mafiosi and contemporary noble robber stories. Contemporary culture has a prominent place for these characters, even if it typically attempts to de-radicalize them. Capitalism tries to make profit on this engagement as it does with many others. However, these figures may be a bit more difficult to contain, due to their connection to the trickster archetype – notoriously hard to contain...

Secondly, the study of alternative organizations shows that they can show an extraordinary transformative potential, while also developing resilience and sustainability. Based on an extensive study, Ewa Bogacz-Wojtanowska[343] proposes that alternative organizations learn remarkably fast by creating nets of action based on co-operation and solidarity. Polish not-for-profit organizations have, since 1989 when they began emerging, been developing very successfully and fulfilling many important social and economic functions, such as drawing in funding for the health care system, supporting education, expanding the practice of local democracy, and much more. They have also developed their own successful system of management based on co-operation among each other and with organizations of other sectors. The studied organizations acquired a number of skills and capabilities such as practices ensuring transparency, structurally cultivating relationships with key stakeholders, financial management procedures, and many others, and they are learning to use them as systems of complementary elements, aimed to help them to adapt to different and changing surroundings. Their own models for leadership and participant cohesion are also developing: they seem to be able to use their unique skills in order to do new things in new ways, not only rely on imitating other organizations, such as, for example, private sector management styles. Thanks to the engagement of participants, they are able to keep a high level of creativity. They also act as promoters of important social causes and guardians of knowledge. However, Bogacz-Wojtanowska holds that co-operation is uniquely the most important among these skills and abilities, as it ascertains internal cohesion, a highly sustainable approach to resource management and establishing and caring for relationships with external stakeholders. By working together they are able to be much more effective in tackling important issues than if they act separately. Organizations help each other out, by engaging people to act for a weaker partner or by mentoring representatives of the other organization. They also readily engage in co-operation with private and public sector organizations, learning from them and developing networks that may prove to be crucial at a certain point in time. For example, they may ask for assistance when they need help with finding a workplace or when they need access to some important resources. When in need they are able to mobilize such help remarkably fast and effectively and from a large variety of partners, from within their own sector and from others.

Similar organizational skills, even if in much more difficult circumstances, are reported by Maria Daskalaki[344] who carried out an extensive study of Greek alternative organizations during the current acute crisis. Even in such extreme conditions, the studied organizations showed extraordinary abilities to mobilize resources and active resistance to what appears as an overpowering order. She tells the tale of two self-organized spaces: a squatted garden and a social centre and shows how they engage in transformative organizing by the interrelated processes of formation of resistance assemblages, social learning and socio-spatial solidarity. She identifies enactment of spontaneous events, or happenings, which she calls *drases,* which are navigated by the organizers to assemble sustainable non-hierarchical structures based on the sharing of ideas and resources. During these drases they also built new relationships and solidarities and planned resistance events. Drases happen unexpectedly and are not planned and the management of them does not mean attempts at control but consists of the ability to use them as catalysts for organizing. They are also used to build social learning platforms in order to create more permanent alternative organizational forms. She concludes that the emerging structures show a striking potential for the enactment of resistance and "the drasis signifies a possibility that something substantial can be made from things that otherwise may have remained invisible or unimagined"[345].

Zofia Łapniewska[346] presents her study of two urban initiatives in Poland and argues that it is possible to reconstitute urban commons by organizing and social activism. The organizers uphold their right to the city and reclaim traditionally existing commons, while extending them and creating a new sense of the common good. The studied grassroots organizations are different and belong to a different urban context. The first is active in a big city and has broad locally political goals. The second is a rather pragmatic initiative, aimed at participation in the decision-making about a fragment of the budget in a small town. However, they are both rooted in a firm belief that citizens have a right to take part in decision-making concerning their city or town and feel compelled to act collectively on this conviction. There is currently a wave of similar initiatives throughout the country and they have achieved certain successes, perhaps more so than other political grassroots initiatives. Łapniewska points out that this may be an institutional seed working on many scales and scopes, they may grow into social movements bringing democracy and giving a new life to the value of the commons.

A food activism project, Occupy the Kitchen[347], run by three organizers since 2016, Franca Formenti, Evelyn Leveghi and Francesca Sironi in Varese, Italy, is an ongoing event with many characteristics of a kind of standing drasis, described by Daskalaki. Evelyn Leveghi has described the project as connected to art and economics, and carried out by research and production. She observes that it aims to expose the contraditions and gaps in the economy and the state of society nowadays by activity that inspires questioning of the status quo and promotes greater awareness. It is an experiment inviting co-experimentation, energizing and encouraging through common engagement in the production, consumption and celebration of food. The activist explained that the project is a reaction to my book *Occupy Management!*[348] and is part of the *Zona Franca* project, and both are under *Foodpower* umbrella, active since 2007.

Asked for a comment on her and her colleagues' project, Franca

Formenti explained:[349]

> My business model is very simple and the real challenge is
> not in producing food with ancient seeds not registered in
> the European catalogue, and therefore irregular. They cannot
> be bought or sold, and so the products made with these also
> cannot be bought or sold. The real challenge is that we are
> having a small activity, and the amount of produced food
> is very small. The concept is fascinating as a metaphor of
> creating a business with elements such as seeds that have not
> been contaminated by capitalism and therefore borderline
> if not completely illegal. I am very happy about this, even
> though it was and is tiring because my life as an artist used
> to be much quieter.
>
> Artists are slow and meditative people, and now my life
> is hectic and demanding. The result is so satisfying that I
> nonetheless am willing to pay for it with constant exhaustion.
> I'm no longer a youngster and my energy is limited.

About her aims and hopes, she said:

> I just hope to be able to organize my take-away to the point
> of becoming a real restaurateur and not always having to
> be present in the kitchen, to have a structure to take care of
> things.
>
> I have two employees, a 20-year-old apprentice who has
> been with me for almost two years and is a skilled chef,
> and a 33-year-old dishwasher. She has been working for me
> for almost two years. With structure, I mean that they are
> learning to be autonomous and the dishwasher is learning
> to cook, shop and organize supplies. My goal is to be able
> to detach myself and concentrate on *Occupy the kitchen!*, my
> other big challenge.
>
> This is about selecting of artists who propose to do

performances in a commercial place as a take-away restaurant where the artist's work is experienced by an audience of customers. So from September 2018 to April 2019 there will be 4 artists who will propose performative work. Now imagine the take-away, where one part of the food is cooked with ancient seeds, giving a voice to the performative art as if it were a gallery that hosts artists.

The current location of the restaurant, a small Italian city, is not ideal from her point of view. She has plans:

Many times I have had the temptation to move Zona Franca in a city like Milan, more receptive and if you want more cosmopolitan, but I have always been held back by the belief that the quality of my life is high because I live in a very beautiful, green town, and the shop is close to my home. Moving to Milan meant to completely change the style of life, for the better at the business level but for the worse for the quality of my life.

So I thought with the other two of my colleagues that we could use Varese, the city where Zona Franca is located, as a kind of gym to understand how to organize performances, menus etc., and then, as a second edition of *Occupy the kitchen!* clone Zona Franca in another city. We could set up a restaurant by renting the kitchen and bringing the tables and chairs. We would present a programme with artists who create performances in the evening, and later we could serve dinner to the guests and the artists as well. We could plan everything for a period of time, for example 10 days or a month, and then disassemble everything and change the city. It would be like musicians or a theatrical troupe on tour.

The idea of this came to her while reading a book:
What I learned by reading Bauman is that human perception

is now so used to the perpetual motion and change, that all the structures and ideas that, for centuries, have been the cornerstones of our existence, are turning into something fluid and precarious. As the internet made musicians precarious, now netflix is also evicting the cinema and making it possible for people to see TV series at home, online. The internet has trained the human mind to be attuned to the continuous flow of images. With a click you move the screen and change the image. This has not only distorted the ability to concentrate in the new generations but also destabilized commercial activities. Any commercial activity, except rare cases, works well at the beginning, then takes a massive drop, because the user is so attached to the idea of incessant change, expecting it all the time, as if life should model itself after the internet.

An excellent example of this is Zara. They are widely known for their low prices, copying designer collections and more. But, in my opinion, the winning card of Zara is that it changes compulsively the merchandise. Every week, or every 10 days at a maximum, they renew, remove, change everything, and the customer's curiosity is caught and awakened. Even though Zara is far from our favourite business model, we have learned from its marketing mode. We are using the same mode at the restaurant: with a constantly changing display of food in our shop-window, and with menus that change every week, always introducing something new, we keep the attention and interest of our customers.

So we have two basic ideas. The first is that of an internet imperialism that glues the person to the screen, turning him or her away from reality. The second is the off-line compulsive need of experiencing everything in motion all the time. I baptized this phenomenon "temporary vision".

Now let's go back to contemporary art. I think it is in crisis, if we talk about painting, installations, sculpture, in short, everything that is static. It may be so because the human mind is now dependent on the continuous renewal of images, on the "temporary vision". But the purest art is always produced by subversives. So, what can art be today and what position can it take that can have a potential to attract attention? Like it usually happens in art history, when a new technological medium appears, as today the internet, art takes an opposite and critical path towards it and then through it.

So let us now consider food. Why is everyone talking about food? Apart from the speculation of the big multinational companies, the conceptual, philosophical reason is that food crosses our bowels, penetrates us. Today, in a moment of great moral crisis, we need introspection, we need to focus on something that is inside us. Food is a metaphor. As well as something very real, very actual. And that is why I work with food.

So, we invite an artist to Zona Franca to work with a performance in the kitchen. We publish a billboard with the program of the four artists for the season from October 2018 to April 2019. We accept reservations. Guests come to visit us as if they were going to a gallery that does not have paintings or sculptures but something that crosses them, something to chew, digest and expel. And then? Then, at the end of the season, we shall go to another city like Milan, Rome, Berlin, London, Sydney.

In each location, also in the various clones of Zona Franca, everything will be sold, from chandeliers, chairs, tables, etc. It will be there and then disappear...Now tell me I am crazy I would like to mix art, activism and business!

Disalienation

Research into alternative organizations reveals that they are able to disalienate work. In an article based on ethnographic research in alternative economic organizations in Poland and the UK co-authored with Jerzy Kociatkiewicz and Martin Parker,[350] we propose that work is an important part of the human being's and the organization's life experience and is connected to the sense of ownership of life (if not always of the means of production). It helps one gain self-respect and make a difference by doing something useful for oneself, other people or the natural environment. Contemporary workplaces do not give any of these things, instead, they seem to be taking away something vital. In Peter Fleming's[351] apt analogy, the neoliberal workplace, be it factory or university, most resembles a forced labour camp.

> Jobs utilize our public imagination and buzz of life, our vested abilities and genuine desire to self-organize, but the net payback is a momentum of subtraction rather than freedom. Worry, fear, anxiety, and a nagging sense of purposelessness tend to result, or what Virno calls a lasting "not feeling at home"[352].

Work is meaningless and alienating, people have no sense of autonomy or agency. This is often per se a strong motive for some people to establish alternative workplaces. The ones we have studied stress the connection between work and personal and societal well-being. The employees find it extremely important that their work constitutes a meaningful form of social participation. Our interviewees felt that, even if the work they were doing was not always interesting or a source of pleasure, they felt in control over their work situation and they had a sense of knowing why they were performing particular tasks. The alternative organizations we studied regularly held meetings where all the important issues of goals and means were discussed and decided upon. The organizations usually offered a living but not opulent wages, and this was regarded as satisfactory. The meaning of work and sense of common good seemed to matter more than just matters of income. Also status did not seem to count more than the belonging to a disalienating endeavour. Our interviewees felt a strong dedication to the organizations' goals, regardless of their positions in the structures (which tended overall to be flat and democratic) or length of involvement. While in common capitalist organizations the organizing principle tends to be subordination, in the disalienating workplaces we have been researching, participation is pivotal. All the organizations in our study aim to make their participants feel at home. Instead of focusing on leisure, as much of the public discourse tends to do, bringing up issues such as work-life balance or lifestyle, the alternative organizations seek to be meaningful in themselves and some are even explicitly intended as exit routes from capitalism. People work together for common emancipation and hope that it can spread to others and gain momentum, until it is regarded as obvious that work has, what Karl Marx[353] called, an affirmative and reciprocal characteristic, being the objectification of the worker's individuality and life, as well as a way of bringing enjoyment and the satisfaction of his or her needs.

Not all alternatives are examples of humane and ethical organizing. Michael Pratt[354] tells an ethnographic story of a direct selling organization (DSO). The participants are not formally employees of the organization but buy its products and then re-sell them, attracting and engaging new participants. If they are successful, they bring themselves up in the organization's structure and enjoy more status and earn a greater income. The whole thing works as a pyramid scheme and much of the organization's activity is focused on the building of morale by the creation of a strong internal culture through such media as meetings, audio and video records, publications and seminars. This material contains lessons about selling techniques and is also suffused with strongly promoted company values. Pratt reports that both the ideas and their intensity reminded him of religious beliefs and evangelical zeal. The organization is an "ideological fortress", offering a complete worldview, guarding itself (and its members) from outside attack. In exchange it demands total identification. Values and spiritual ideas are not used to offer consolation or hope of redemption but are meant to attach people more tightly to the organization. They are also strategically linked with economic values: a good parent is the one who nourishes the relationship between their family and God, and earns money as a distributor. Everything, including family and friendship, is in its essence linked with economic values. A person who is not successful is castigated as having put in too little effort or having too little faith. Protests are framed as the work of the devil. This worldview makes this organization total and complete, even if no physical barriers are erected – the mental and spiritual walls are put up and any gaps in them are sealed.

Martin Parker[355] makes a case for the need of business beyond capitalism, in social-democratic society, and argues that small business is more environmentally sustainable and more resilient nationally and locally, and also has a potential to develop more economic democracy. They are not necessarily just a kind of economic plankton, as there is an abundance of evidence that such organizations are very good at networking (which Ewa Bogacz-Wojtanowska also emphasizes in her work), and able to create strong and vibrant ecosystems throughout regions, and perhaps even whole countries. They are good at sharing resources and co-operation, which supports lasting innovation. Parker ponders the question: "What sorts of policy or ecosystem changes would be necessary to encourage alternative businesses to grow?"[356] The left and Critical Management Studies have been for long focusing on the dangers of market managerialism and on the critique of economic injustice, and avoiding constructive propositions, thus making some ground for the right to keep a reputation of being more competent in economic issues. However, the economy could be re-designed to work for the common good. Parker is taking part in the work of a UK socialist think tank set up by the Labour Party and his area of expertise concerns alternative organizations. He suggests that big corporations should cease to act as a measure for the health of the economy, as they are a minority type of organization, employ less people than small businesses, and are much less beneficial for the building of a just society. The attention of policy makers should be directed to the latter and away from the former. There should be tax incentives to sell businesses to employee trusts or co-ops. Employees should be given the possibility to buy, if there is an offer. Employee-owned businesses should be given priority as government suppliers. Local governments should be encouraged to support local economic alternatives. There should be viable options to seek funding from the financial sectors that address the needs of small businesses. The taxation systems should be adapted to encourage economic democracy. It is also necessary to engage in more and more substantial research and thinking dedicated to alternatives and to make business schools tackle this area instead of the current almost exclusive focus on corporate managerialism. The research should offer broad ideas, propositions of how to embed alternative organizations in a socio-economic context that would speak to the imagination of important stakeholders. It should also propose concrete viable solutions for concrete countries and regions.

I asked Martin Parker for a reflection on how he sees the relationship between hope and such organizations and the story below is his answer to my question.

Martin Parker: The Hope for Something Other

I think "hope" probably begins with a consciousness of boredom, of dull inevitability stretching into the future. The repetitions of the present are often so deadening in their rhythm and tone that it is easy enough to drift into daydreams in which something else might happen. Fantasy, romance and glamour are ways of escape from this boredom, and so are science fiction, utopianism and forms of radical politics that imagine a different future. These are methods of thinking and doing within which strangeness might erupt and lives lived inattentively become present to hand.

In terms of organizing, the dominant forms in the global north (which can be summarized as "market managerial") seek to produce a future in which the value produced by all production, consumption and exchange is captured by gigantic hierarchical structures. The language of "care", "passion", "choice" and so on, routinely expressed by those who do the marketing and public relations for large organizations, is no more than an invitation to this capture. This, it seems to me, is boring in the sense that it produces a future of more of the same. More inequality; more advertising; more carbon emissions; more hierarchy; more consumption; more waste; more dull jobs; more claims to be responsible, to care, to be passionate about choice. This is an organizational monoculture, a predictable landscape in which a fundamental repetition is camouflaged by bright colours, smiling faces and a soundtrack by someone who sounds like Coldplay.

This is what leads me and plenty of others to have daydreams about an alternative future, one in which a variety of forms of organizing produce difference. My bet is on a bestiary of forms, on an irreducible pluralism which generates resilient and distinct economies. I think that this means that there will be a tendency towards the small, the local, partly because giganticism erases distinctiveness when it swallows it, but also because shorter supply chains and meaningful senses of responsibility to human and non-human others require proximity. Just as we might travel to other places and discover different flora, fauna and landscape, so would I like to think that we could discover organizational variety in different places too.

This means pushing against the entropy that market managerialism routinely generates on a global level. The same shouty global brands and celebrities, the same foods and products moved around in shipping containers, and even the same language. This is boring because it seems to suggest that our collective future is one which everywhere and for everyone will be the same. (And all the while, the planet warms.) For me, hope is the whisper of the strange, of existence and experience which is not a marketed cliché, or part of an engineered cradle of dull lies.

Coda: In praise of margins

"Things fall apart; the centre cannot hold," proclaimed William Butler Yeats in his much-cited poem, "The second coming"[357]. The image of the Apocalypse depicted in the poem is that of magnificent collapse, "the falcon cannot hear the falconer", a tide has come loose, chaos is released upon humanity. The poet asks whether a revelation is at hand and turns his eyes towards Bethlehem, the marginal place where the Messiah had once been born. While the centre collapses, we look to the margins for a second coming to bring us hope for a future worth living in.

The centre is all about power, it is where knowledge is moulded and cast in structures and institutions, where it is decided which truth is to be considered valid and effective. The centre then consequently centrifugally disposes of what is false or just not binding, not authorized or legitimate by the system. While the centre becomes increasingly stable, it loses its diversity, sacrificed to the stabilization. Yet, as the systems theory[358] is telling us, it is from the margins and thanks to the existence of diverse potentialities that the system acquires the ability to regenerate and renew itself. A system that has become too pure, too monolithic, too well-ordered around one or two polarized modes is one doomed to death. Its truths become devoid of the living variety of human experience; its cannons impervious to creativity. What we witness today in the social world is a strong illustration of this state of things. The coagulation of institutions around the Thatcherite dogma of "no alternative", known as TINA, a strong polarization of politics around options that do not seem to be able to be either reconciled or bring in any truly new ideas, the thinning out of social imagination to the point of a disbanding of future[359] create a very strong and stark image of inevitability and absolute power. At the same time, the system does not even deliver what it promises – growth is slacking and is not rational. By the way, these issues become insignificant as compared to their side effects: growing social problems, global poverty, increasing injustice[360], and economic crises on a magnificent scale[361]. The system, as monolithic as it seems, appears to be intrinsically flawed. It has ceased to be able to regenerate itself, to use crises as an opportunity to reinvent itself, instead, it only seems able to repeat the same "solutions" that have caused its problems in the first place – from a systems point of view, a sure sign of morbidity[362]. Neoliberalism is, to me, not an ideology, not a system, not an approach to economy or politics. It is a final, deadly stage of life of a huge socio-economic system –modern capitalism, a kind of systemic dementia. There are compelling signs of the system having lost its ability to regenerate itself, of *autopoiesis*[363]. The omnipresent imagery of zombies in media, culture and social sciences seems to reflect a collective imagination in a time so pertinently described by Antonio Gramsci[364]:

The old is dying and the new cannot be born. In this interregnum a great variety of morbid symptoms can appear.

What is most needed now – new ideas, utopias, alternatives – is also most conspicuously absent from a centre that has grown into a magnificent monolith, the only visible social reality for most of humanity. It is either the raw violence of vision of alt right or the increasingly more open false promises of neoliberal moguls; either the ugly communities built on exclusion and xenophobia or the globalizing drive, ready to open all borders to capital but not human beings; either prejudice elevated to virtue or virtue presented as a façade and façade turned into virtue proper... envy or greed. The choice seems to be not so much limited as oppressive and claustrophobic.

And yet alternatives exist, as I hope to have revealed in this book, even if but a little of the superlative abundance. They are where they have been pushed out by the centrifugal force of the centre maximizing its power, and where all new ideas tend to be born – in the margins. Organization theorist and one of the founding mothers of humanistic management, Heather Höpfl[365], used to say that if you want to find future modes of organizing, you should look to the margins, not to the centre, especially in times of turbulence and uncertainty. Extrapolation is, at this moment, illusory, a kind of systemic life-support equipment that only prolongs the inevitable. It is a huge system and it has been defining social life for decades and centuries, so it may endure long in this lifeless shape, until cut off by a cataclysmic event like another major ecological disaster or yet one more outbreak of urgent civil unrest. Or until it just implodes – the centre does not hold and, one day, it will empty itself of any life. The social abhors a vacuum, and all the current trajectories seem to point in precisely that direction – a workplace without workers (they will be replaced by robots), driverless cars, classes taught by holograms, empty homes-investments, policies without compassion, society without solidarity. As modern as it all seems, it is empty of humans, human life, human suffering and love. A system with a centre like this will implode all by itself. No seeds of the new can be found there. No, to find these, we need to look to the margins, read the books less cited, walk the roads less taken, study the organizations less fashionable, explore the theories less popular. I have shared, in this book, some of the ideas and insights found on the electrifying peripheries of organization studies but I do not claim this to be a closed book, a recipe for hope, or thesis on hope. Quite the contrary, it is my modest contribution to the common repository of marginal knowledge for a meaningful organizational future.

It is what Titus Flamininus did in his time. Himself a marginal hero of history, not very well known, not universally acclaimed as the author of grand ideas, he spent his life in a devotion to the marginal. He defended the Greek culture and its right to be expressed, as well as propagating it among the inhabitants of what was then the grand centre – Rome. Thanks to modest heroes, recyclers of Greek ideas, even though the structures and institutions did not survive the apocalypse of conquest and centralization of the emerging empire, the symbols and values did, reused for Roman, and then Christian, Arabic and modern purposes. They were able to unite and kindle sparks of inspiration. It is important, because culture is our most potentially humane aspect. The human ape is not a kind animal: it relishes violence, it is occasionally cruel for no particular reason, it thrives on hierarchies of power; it is greedy and egoistic. Culture brings out and develops the other side of humanity, one that involves higher feelings, solidarity, civility and hope. Yes, hope, that uniquely human strand of insubordination, the willingness to forsake comfort for something that is out of reach yet, to forsake gain for risk. One may say it is hope itself that draws us towards the margins, even though we could securely slumber in the centre – in search of what is impossible, non-existent, implausible, the Grail, Utopia, redemption. To hope is truly human.

Looking at images of the mind-boggling vastness of space, galaxies, distant suns, one cannot but notice how marginal our planet is. And concentrating just on planet Earth and its history, it is hard not to realize how marginal the human presence is in the face of millennia, of billions of years that this history extends to. We are marginal creatures in a marginal world. If one is a believer, it is perhaps a consolation to realize this, together with the strong prohibition on pride in most religions[366], that God likes margins. If He did not, He would not send His Son to be born in a poor uneducated family in Bethlehem, and would not abide Him to promise to the last that they shall be the first. He would not send His holy prophet Muhammed to teach in the faraway desert, to people far from the political centres of the contemporary world. He would not have chosen a small people for His covenant, often dispersed, sometimes enslaved, occasionally stateless. He and she would not inspire sadhus to go into self-imposed exile from the bustle of life. No, God obviously likes margins. And if one is agnostic or an atheist one may perhaps stoically observe that we, humans, are but a piece of dust in the face of the Universe, less than that, even and yet – as Prince Hamlet exclaims: What a piece of work is man! To be human is worthy not despite but because of how insignificant we are, and yet – how great our hopes and dreams are. If we are to pass on our humanity without resorting to a regress to the rule of atavisms, we need to develop ways of finding and recycling cultural ideas, symbols, values where they are to be found. We, marginal creatures, need to set out into the margins of the system, the dust roads of culture. Titus Flamininus is something to be.

What has crashed and fallen, is fallen and will not spring into life anew. The structures that have been accompanying us and our ancestors for centuries are now in ruins and no amount of positive thinking, or affirmations, no army of energetic psychopath CEOs, and no mind-boggling amount of rules and regulations will change this. But we can make it easier for ourselves in the future, when we will try to erect new structures able to carry the culture of collective action. It will be either a slow process following total dissipation, going back to barbarity and beginning again. Or finding a common ground of values and ideas that can be shared and that inspire the creation of a new social system and its parts. It depends on what we do today and not so much on the centre, which is slowly drifting towards oblivion, in one way or another. It will depend on what we find and construct in the margins, to be used by ourselves or our successors. This is a layer of marginal meaning that Walter Benjamin[367] calls messianic time: the immediate, experienced; meaning left behind in history can be retrieved and redeemed. Messianic moments are hidden underneath dead linear time, which is the time measured by clocks, found in rules, regulations and management documents. There are revolutionary moments present in the margins of history, awaiting redemption.

Fall[368]

And if we ever were to be forgiven,
please let it be before the winter arrives,
while we have not yet settled
for the obviously clear
and when betrayal is still betrayal,
even when it is all clean and crisp.
If redemption comes,
let it be in autumn,
in the pouring rain,
in the mud.

Endnotes

i   Anthrakia (Monika Kostera) (2019) *I am not Magritte*. Cardiff: Wordcatcher, forthcoming.

1   Plutarch (1921) *Parallel Lives,* published in Vol. X of the Loeb Classical Library edition, retrieved from: http://penelope.uchicago.edu/Thayer/E/Roman/Texts/Plutarch/Lives/Flamininus*.html

2   Rene Pfeilschifter (2005) *Titus Quinctius Flamininus: Untersuchungen zur romischen Griechenlandpolitik.* Göttingen: Vandenhoeck & Ruprecht.

3   Zygmunt Bauman (2012) "Times of Interregnum", *Ethics and Global Politics*, 5/1: 49-56.

4   Zygmunt Bauman (2017) *Retrotopia.* Cambridge: Polity Press.

5   Karl E. Weick, (1979) *The Social Psychology of Organizing.* Reading: Addison-Wesley.

6   Karl E. Weick, (1995) *Sensemaking in Organizations.* Thousand Oaks, CA: Sage.

7   James G. March (1999) *The Pursuit of Organizational Intelligence.* Oxford: Blackwell.

8   James G. March and Johan P. Olsen (1989) *Rediscovering Institutions.* Free Press: New York.

9   Zygmunt Bauman (2000) *Liquid Modernity.* Cambridge: Polity Press.

10   Wendy Brown (2006) "American Nightmare: Neoliberalism, Neoconservatism, and De-Democratization", *Political Theory*, 34(6), 690-714.

11   Peter Fleming (2014) *Resisting Work: The Corporatization of Life and its Discontents.* Philadelphia: Temple University Press.

12   David Graeber (2018) *Bullshit Jobs: A Theory.* London: Allen Lane.

13   Carl Cederström and Peter Fleming (2012) *Dead Man Working.* Hants: Zero Books.

14   Wolfgang Streeck (2017) *How will Capitalism End? Essays on a Failing System.* London: Verso.

15 Peter Fleming (2017) *The Death of Homo Economicus: Work, Debt and the Myth of Endless Accumulation.* London: Pluto Press.

16 Peter Bloom and Carl Rhodes (2018) *CEO Society: The Corporate Takeover of Everyday Life.* London: Zed Books.

17 Arlie Russell Hochschild (201) *The Outsourced Self: Intimate Life in Market Times.* New York: Metropolitan Books.

18 Adam Tooze (2018) *Crashed: How a Decade of Financial Crises Changed the World.* London: Allen Lane.

19 Naomi Klein (2017) *No is not Enough: Defeating the New Shock Politics.* London: Penguin.

20 *Turning and turning in the widening gyre*
   The falcon cannot hear the falconer;
   Things fall apart; the centre cannot hold;
   Mere anarchy is loosed upon the world,
   The blood-dimmed tide is loosed, and everywhere
   The ceremony of innocence is drowned;
   The best lack all conviction, while the worst
   Are full of passionate intensity. (William Butler Yeats, "The second coming", fragment)

21 One of the few examples is oko.press, an independent Polish internet-based investigative journalism project. The incomplete report can be accessed here: https://oko.press/university-of-warsaw-is-under-occupation-stop-the-anti-democratic-academic-reforms/ It only mentions one of the sites of the protests (Warsaw).

22 March (1999), *op. cit.*

23 Patti Smith (2017) *Devotion.* New Haven: Yale University Press.

24 Zygmunt Bauman with Benedetto Vecchi (2004) *Identity.* London: Polity.

25 Bauman (2017) op. cit.

26 By Charles Perrow (1991) "A Society of Organizations". *Theory and Society* 20, 725–62.

27 Vaclav Havel (1990) *Disturbing the Peace: A Conversation with Karel Hvizdala.* New York: Vintage, 181-2.

28 Zygmunt Bauman (2017) "O wszystkim, co najważniejsze",

wyborcza.pl, retrieved from http://wyborcza.pl/51,75398,21222206. html?i=0

29 Friedrich Nietzsche (2008) *The Birth of Tragedy*. Oxford: OUP.

30 Ruth Benedict (1993) *Patterns of Culture*. Boston: Houghton Mifflin.

31 Inga Grześczak (2002) Ścieżki śródziemnomorskie. Warszawa: Wiedza Powszechna.

32 Melvyn Bragg (2002) *In our Time*, BBC Radio 4, retrieved from https://www.bbc.co.uk/programmes/p00548h4

33 However, the Romans did not destroy cultures they conquered, they were much more careful and respectful towards their values than today's victors. The task we face today may be more difficult than it was in ancient times. I would like to thank Piotr Ahmad for this insight.

34 Weick (1979), op. cit., 3.

35 Bracketing means taking something out of the main stream of perception.

36 Karl E. Weick (1995) *Sensemaking in Organizations*. Thousand Oaks, CA: Sage.

37 John Law (1994) *Organizing Modernity*. Oxford: Routledge.

38 Nils Brunsson, (1985) *The Irrational Organization: Irrationality as a Basis for Organizational Action and Change*. Chichester, UK: John Wiley.

39 Weick (1979), op. cit.

40 Barbara Czarniawska-Joerges (1992) *Exploring Complex Organizations: A Cultural Perspective*. Newbury Park: SAGE, 32.

41 Mary Jo Hatch (1983) "The Dynamics of Organizational Culture". *Academy of Management Review* 18/4, 657-93.

42 Susan Wright (1994) "Culture in Anthropology and Organizational Studies". in: Susan Wright (ed.) *Anthropology of Organizations*. London: Routledge, 1-31.

43 Paul J. DiMaggio and Walter W. Powell (1991) "Introduction" in: Walter W. Powell and Paul J. DiMaggio (ed.) *The New Institutionalism in Organizational Analysis*. Chicago: Chicago University Press, 1-38.

44 Richard W. Scott (1995) *Institutions and Organizations*. Thousand

Oaks: Sage.

45 Guje Sevón (1998) "Organizational Imitation and Identity Transformation". in: Nils Brunsson and Johan P. Olsen (ed.) *Organizing Organizations*. Bergen: Fagbokförlaget, 237-78.

46 Jenny Helin and Marie-Jose Avenier (2016) "Inquiring into Arresting Moments over Time: Towards an Understanding of Stability within Change", *Scandinavian Journal of Management*, 32, 142-9.

47 DiMaggio and Powell (1991), op. cit.

48 Sven-Erik Sjöstrand (1998) "Företagsledning" in: Barbara Czarniawska *Organisationsteori på svenska*. Malmö: Liber, 22-42.

49 See for example Barbara Czarniawska-Joerges and Pierre Guillet de Monthoux (1994) (eds.) *Good Novels, Better Management: Reading Organizational Realities*. Chur: Harwood.

50 See e.g. Heather Höpfl (2000d) "On Being Moved", *Studies in Cultures, Organizations and Societies*, 6(1): 15-34.

51 Monika Kostera (2006) "The Narrative Collage as Research Method", *Storytelling, Self, Society*, 2/2: 5-27.

52 There also exists a practitioner-oriented variation of the method, proposed by Henrietta Nilson, where the respondents are requested to contribute with stories, images and music, and the aim is to, first, explore and then animate the creative potential of the organization. Henrietta Nilson (2009) *Henriettas Collage: Kreativa kvinnor i familjeföretag*. Växjö: Drivkraft.

53 Monika Kostera (2012) *Organizations and Archetypes*. Cheltenham: Edward Elgar.

54 Roman Ingarden (1960) *O dziele literackim: Badania z pogranicza antologii, teorii języka i filozofii*. Warszawa: PWN.

55 Story translated from the Polish original by Klaudyna Cwynar.

56 William Blake (1790) *The Marriage of Heaven and Hell*. Retrieved on 18/7/2018 from https://www.bartleby.com/235/253.html

57 Aristotle (2009) *Nicomachean Ethics*. Oxford: OUP.

58 Ibid., 28.

59 Isaac Newton (2016) *The Principia: Mathematical Principles of Natural*

Philosophy. transl. Bernard Cohen and Julia Budenz, Oakland: University of California Press.

60 *Cogito ergo sum*, René Descartes (1996) *Discourse on the Method*. Ed. John Cottingham, Cambridge: CUP.

61 For example, Stefan Amsterdamski (1983) *Nauka a porządek świata*. Warszawa: PWN.

62 Immanuel Kant (2007) *Critique of Pure Reason*. London: Penguin.

63 Ibid., 635, original emphasis.

64 Ibid., 636.

65 Ibid., 636.

66 Pseudonym.

67 Norman Bowie (1999) *Business Ethics: A Kantian Perspective*. Malden: Blackwell.

68 Monika Kostera (2016) "Humanistic Management", in: Barbara Czarniawska (ed.) *A Research Agenda for Management and Organization Studies*, Cheltenham: Edward Elgar, 48-58.

69 Terence Collins and Greg Latemore (2015) "Philosophising at Work: An Agenda for Discussion", *Philosophy of Management*, 2(2), 55-66.

70 Ibid., 56.

71 Ibid., 58.

72 Frits Schipper (2009) "Excess of Rationality? About Rationality, Emotion and Creativity. A Contribution to the Philosophy of Management and Organization", *Tamara Journal*, 7 (7.4.), 161-76.

73 Ibid., 162.

74 Peter Case, Robert French and Peter Simpson (2012) "From *theoria* to theory: Leadership without Contemplation", *Organization*, 19 (3), 345-61.

75 Peter Case and Jonathan Gosling (2007) "Wisdom of the Moment: Pre-modern Perspectives on Organizational Action", *Social Epistemology*, 21 (2), 87-111.

76 Ibid., 96.

77 Ibid., 106.

78 Ann L. Cunliffe (2009) "The Philosopher Leader: On Rationalism,

Ethics and Reflexivity – a Critical Perspective to Teaching Leadership", *Management Learning*, 40(1), 87–101.

79   Ibid., 94.

80   If in any doubt at all about the seriousness of the situation, see books such as George Monbiot (2017), *Out of the Wreckage: A New Politics for an Age of Crisis*. London: Verso and Naomi Klein (2017) *No is not Enough: Defeating the New Shock Politics*. London: Penguin.

81   Stephen Allen, Ann L. Cunliffe and Mark Easterby-Smith (2017) "Understanding Sustainability through the Lens of Ecocentric Radical-reflexivity: Implications for Management Education", *Journal of Business Ethics*, DOI 10.1007/s10551-016-3420-3

82   Ibid., np.

83   Ehh, it is true, alas…for a critique see e.g. Aaron Vasintjan (2018) "The Shitty New Communist Futurism", *Entitle Blog – A Collaborative Writing Project on Political Ecology*, retrieved from https://entitleblog.org/2018/01/25/the-shitty-new-communist-futurism/

84   Christopher Grey (2003) "The Fetish of Change", *Tamara Journal for Critical Organization Inquiry*, 2(2), 1-19.

85   Zygmunt Bauman and Tim May (2001) *Thinking Sociologically*. Oxford: Blackwell.

86   Ibid., 180.

87   Jonathan H. Turner, Leonard Beeghley and Chalres H. Powers (2012) *The Emergence of Sociological Theory*. London: SAGE.

88   Ibid.

89   Frederick Engels (2017) *Ludwig Feuerbach and the End of Classical German Philosophy*. edited by Sankar Srinivasan, India: LeoPard Books.

90   See e.g. Turner et al. (2012), op. cit., for more juxtapositions between Marx and other founders of sociological thought.

91   C. Wright Mills (1959) *The Sociological Imagination*. London: Oxford University Press.

92   Bauman (2017) *Retrotopia*, op cit.

93   Ibid., 166.

94 Jerzy Kociatkiewicz and Monika Kostera (2014) (Eds.) *Liquid Organization: Zygmunt Bauman and Organization Theory*. Oxford: Routledge.

95 Ibid.

96 Zygmunt Bauman (2017) "Has the Future a Left?", *Soundings*, 35, retrieved from https://www.lwbooks.co.uk/soundings/35/has-future-left

97 David Lyon (2017) "Bauman's Sociology of Hope", *Cultural Politics*, 13(3), 296-9, DOI: 10.1215/17432197-4211266

98 Ibid., 298.

99 Martin Parker (2015) "Between Sociology and the Business School: Critical Studies of Work, Employment and Organization in the UK", *The Sociological Review*, 63, 162–80, DOI: 10.1111/1467-954X.12166

100 For story in context, see Parker (2015), ibid.

101 Stewart Clegg and Caren Baumeler (2010) "From Iron Cages to Liquid Modernity in Organization Analysis", *Organization Studies*, 31(12), 1713-33.

102 Ibid., 1728.

103 Andrew Brown, Martin Kornberger, Stewart Clegg and Chris Carter (2010) "'Invisible Walls' and 'Silent Hierarchies': A Case Study of Power Relations in an Architecture Firm", *Human Relations*, 63(4), 525-49.

104 Ibid., 540.

105 Martin Parker (2008) "Eating with the Mafia: Belonging and Violence", *Human Relations*, 61(7), 989–1006.

106 Tâna Silva, Miguel Pina e Cunha, Stewart Clegg, Pedro Neves, Arménio Rego and Ricardo Rodrigues (2014) "Smells Like Team Spirit: Opening a Paradoxical Black Box", *Human Relations*, 67(3), 287-310.

107 Ibid., 305.

108 Stewart Clegg (forthcoming) "Liquefying Modernity and Organization Studies", *Organization Studies*.

109 Ibid., np.

110 Wilhelm Wundt (1975) *An Introduction to Psychology*. New York:

Arno Press, 1.

111 Maslow, Abraham (1968) *Toward a Psychology of Being*. New York: Van Nostrand.

112 Jung, (1990) *The Archetypes and the Collective Unconscious*. (Collected Works, Vol. 9) Princeton University Press.

113 Ibid., 33.

114 Roland David Laing and Aaron Esterson (1964) *Sanity, Madness and the Family: Families of Schizophrenics*. Harmondsworth: Penguin.

115 Mihaly Csikszentmihalyi (1990) *Flow: The Psychology of Optimal Experience*. New York: Harper and Row.

116 Else Ouweneel, Pascale Le Blanc, Wilmar Schaufeli and Corine van Wijhe (2012) "Good Morning, Good Day: A Diary Study on Positive Emotions, Hope, and Work Engagement", *Human Relations*, 65(9), 1129-54.

117 Stephen Fineman (2006) "On being Positive: Concerns and Counterpoints", *Academy of Management Review*, 31/2, 270-91.

118 Ibid. 270.

119 Ibid., 275.

120 Yiannis Gabriel (1998) "Psychoanalytic Contributions to the Study of the Emotional Life of Organizations", *Administration & Society*, 30/3, 292-315.

121 Ibid., 308.

122 Ibid., 309.

123 Ibid., 311.

124 Marianna Fotaki, Susan Long and Howard S. Schwartz (2012) "What Can Psychoanalysis Offer Organization Studies Today? Taking Stock of Current Developments and Thinking about Future Directions", *Organization Studies* 33(9), 1105-20.

125 Jonathan Gosling and Peter Case (2013) "Social Dreaming and Ecocentric Ethics: Sources of Non-rational Insight in the Face of Climate Change Catastrophe", *Organization*, 20 (5), 705-21.

126 Manfred Kets de Vries (2006) "The Spirit of Despotism: Understanding the Tyrant Within", *Human Relations*, 59(2): 195–220.

127 Ibid., 196.

128 Ibid., 212.

129 Burkard Sievers (1994) *Work, Death and Life Itself: Essays on Management and Organization*. Berlin: Walter de Gruyter.

130 George A. Kelly (1963) *A Theory of Personality*. New York: Norton, 95.

131 Ibid., 98.

132 Miller Mair (1988) "Psychology as Storytelling", *International Journal of Personal Construct Psychology*, 1(1), 133.

133 Dorota Bourne, email interview.

134 Dorota Bourne, email interview.

135 Arystoteles (1989) *Poetyka*. (*Poetics*) Wrocław: Ossolineum.

136 Umberto Eco (1973*) Dzieło otwarte: Forma i nieokreśloność w poetykach współczesnych*. (*Opera aperta: Forma e indeterminazione nelle poetiche contemporanee*). Warszawa: Czytelnik.

137 Umberto Eco (1990) *The Limits of Interpretation*. Bloomington, Indiana: Indiana University Press.

138 Michel De Certeau (1986) *Heterologies, Discourse on the Other*. Manchester: Manchester University Press.

139 Christpher Caudwell (1946) *Illusion and Reality, a Study of the Sources of Poetry*. London: Lawrence and Wishart.

140 Jalaluddin Rumi (1995) "If You are Seeking…" *Elephant Journal* retrieved from https://www.elephantjournal.com/2017/07/13-rumi-poems-to-awaken-the-love-within-us/

141 Heather Höpfl (1995) "Organisational Rhetoric and the Threat of Ambivalence", *Studies in Cultures, Organizations and Societies*, 1(2): 175-87.

142 Heather Höpfl (1994) "Learning by Heart: The Rules of Rhetoric and the Poetics of Experience", *Management Learning*, 25(3): 463-74.

143 Höpfl (1995), op. cit.

144 Joanna Średnicka (2018) *Organizacja, wspólnota, bunt. Jak mity romantyczne kształtują współpracę w przedsiębiorstwie czasów transformacji*. Doctoral dissertation, Kraków: Uniwersytet Jagielloński.

145 Höpfl (1995), op. cit.

146 Höpfl (1995), op. cit., 176.

147 John Burnside (2006) "A Science of Belonging: Poetry as Ecology", in: Robert Crawford (ed.) *Contemporary Poetry and Contemporary Science*, Oxford: OUP, 91-109.

148 Burnside (2006), op.cit., 95.

149 Höpfl (1995), op. cit.

150 On business talk and, indeed, business bullshit, as a rhetorical managerial strategy see Andre Spicer (2017) *Business Bullshit*. London: Routledge.

151 Monika Kostera (2000) "A Letter from the Empty Stage", *Studies in Cultures, Organizations, and Societies*, 6/1, 1-5.

152 Peter Brook (1990) *The Empty Space*. London: Penguin, 157.

153 Kostera (2000), op.cit., 2.

154 Arnold van Gennep (1909/1960) *The Rites of Passage*. Chicago: University of Chicago Press; Erving Goffman (1959) *The Presentation of Self in Everyday Life*. New York: Random House; Victor Turne (1974) *Dramas, Fields, and Metaphors: Symbolic Action in Human Society*. Ithaca NY: Cornell University Press.

155 Victor Turner (1969) *The Ritual Process: Structure and Anti-Structure*. Ithaca NY: Cornell University Press.

156 Höpfl (2002c), op. cit.

157 Höpfl (2002c), op. cit. 18.

158 John Ruskin (2005) *Modern Painters*. Adamant Media.

159 John Berger (2008) *Ways of Seeing*. London: Penguin.

160 Ibid., 8.

161 John Berger (1972) *Ways of Seeing*. (first edition) London: Penguin.

162 John Berger (1983) "Caravaggio: A Contemporary View", *Studio International*, 196(998), http://timothyquigley.net/vcs/berger-carav aggio.pdf

163 John Berger (1993) *The Sense of Sight*. New York: Vintage, 8-9.

164 John Berger (2011) *Bento's Sketchbook: How Does the Impulse to Draw Something Begin?* New York: Pantheon, 87.

165 Pierre Guillet de Monthoux, (1998) *Konstföretaget: Mellan*

spektakelkultur och kulturspektakel. Stockholm: Korpen.

166 Pierre Guillet de Monthoux (1993) *Det sublimas konstnärliga ledning: Estetik, konst och företag.* Stockholm: Nerenius & Santerus.

167 Ibid., 4.

168 Ceri Watkins, Ian King and Stephen Linstead (2006) "Introduction: Art of Management and Organisation Conference Series", *Culture and Organization,* 12/1, s. 1-2.

169 Stephen Linstead and Heather Höpfl (2000) "Introduction". in: S. Linstead and Heather Höpfl (ed.) *The Aesthetics of Organization.* London, Thousand Oaks, New Delhi: Sage, s. 1-11.

170 Stefan Svallfors (2015) *Kreativitetens människa: Om konsten att ställa sig I hornet och vikten att vårda sina fiender.* Stockholm: Santerus.

171 Stefan Meisek and Daved Barry (2016) "Organizational Studios: Enabling Innovation", in: Ulla Johansson Sköldberg, Jill Woodilla and Ariane Berthoin Antal (eds) *Artistic Interventions in Organizations.* London: Routledge, 225-37.

172 Peter Pelzer (2006) "Art for Management's Sake? A Doubt", *Culture and Organization,* 12/1, s. 65-77.

173 Meisek and Barry (2016), op. cit.

174 Ibid., 229, Interviewee I.2, manager service.

175 Ibid., 228, Interviewee I.1, manager law.

176 Ibid., 231.

177 Ibid., 234.

178 Tobert Stasinki and Pierre Guillet de Monthoux (2017) (eds) *SSE Art Initiative.* Stockholm: SSE.

179 Ibid.

180 Pierre Guillet de Monthoux (2017) "A Word from the Director", in: Robert Stasinski and Pierre Guillet de Monthoux (eds) *SSE Art Initiative.* Stockholm: SSE, 7.

181 Daniel Mendelsohn (2015) "Hearing Sappho", *The New Yorker,* 12 March. Retrieved from https://www.newyorker.com/books/page-turner/hearing-sappho

182 Victor Hugo (1864), *William Shakespeare.* Retrieved from https://fr.wikisource.org/wiki/William_Shakespeare_(Victor_Hugo)/I/

II#IV

183 Ibid.

184 Charles Avison (1775) *An Essay on Musical Expression*. London: Lockyer Davis. Retrieved from http://hz.imslp.info/files/imglnks/usimg/4/4e/IMSLP59385-PMLP121821-Avison_essay_on_musical_expression.pdf

185 Ibid., 19.

186 Terri Paglush (2017) "What is Music? Music Defined by Musicians", *Music House School of Music*, 18 April, retrieved from https://www.musichouseschool.com/what-is-music-music-defined-by-musicians

187 Ibid.

188 Ibid.

189 There is currently a vibrant movement among organizational theorists taking place in the margins of the discourse of the discipline, as a counterweight to the increasingly formulaic research dissemination – see for example Mats Alvesson and Yannis Gabriel (2013) "Beyond Formulaic Research: In Praise of Greater Diversity in Organizational Research and Publications", *Academy of Management Learning and Education*, 12(2), 245-63. An excellent example of how inspiring and vital this wave is can be found in the special issue edited by Sarah Gilmore, Nancy Harding, Jenny Helin and Alison Pullen (2019) "Writing Differently: *Management Learning*, 50(1). All the articles are well worth slow reading. I warmly recommend reading them on paper, not online.

190 Tommy Jensen and Johan Sandström (2018) *Organizing Rocks*. Retrieved from http://www.organizingrocks.org/

191 Ibid.

192 Michael Humphreys, Andrew Brown and Mary Jo Hatch (2003) "Is Ethnography Jazz?" *Organization*, 10/1, 5-31.

193 Ibid., 8.

194 Ibid.

195 Ibid., 13.

196 Mary Jo Hatch (1999) "Exploring the Empty Spaces of Organizing:

How Improvisational Jazz Helps Redescribe Organizational Structure", *Organization Studies*, 20/1, 75-100.

197 Daniel Ericsson (2018) *Tonvigande entreprenörskap: Opera på småländska*. Lund: Studentlitteratur.

198 Yes, you know exactly what it is – the birthplace of IKEA.

199 See e.g. Daniel Ericsson (2019) "Technologies of the Commune: A Bridge over Troubled Water?" in: Daniel Ericsson and Monica Kostera (eds.) *Organizing Hope*. Cheltenham: Edward Elgar, forthcoming.

200 Yiannis Gabriel (2018) *Stories, Music, Psychoanalysis, Politics, Reviews, the Odd Cooking Recipe...*blog, retrieved at: http://www.yiannisgabriel.com/

201 Yiannis Gabriel (2017) "Leadership in Opera: Romance, Betrayal, Strife and Sacrifice". *Organization Studies*, 13(1), 5-19.

202 Ibid., 6.

203 Ibid., 7.

204 Herodotus (2003) *The Histories*. London: Penguin.

205 Ibid., 3.

206 Georg Wilhelm Friedrich Hegel (2001) *The Philosophy of History*. Kitchener: Batoche Books, https://socialsciences.mcmaster.ca/econ/ugcm/3ll3/hegel/history.pdf

207 Ibid., 14.

208 Ibid., 17.

209 Walter Benjamin (2005) *On the Concept of History*. Accessed on 26.05.2017 at https://www.marxists.org/reference/archive/benjamin/1940/history.htm

210 Walter Benjamin (1999) "Theses on the Philosophy of History" in: *Illuminations*. London: Pimlico, 254.

211 Ibid., 264.

212 Hermann Hesse (2012) *Steppenwolf*. London: Penguin.

213 Roy Stager Jacques (2006) "History, Historiography and Organization Studies: The Challenge and the Potential", *Management & Organizational History*, 1:1, 31-49.

214 Harry Braverman (1974) *Labour and Monopoly Capital: The*

Degradation of Work in the Twentieth Century. New York: Monthly Review Press.

215 Roy Jacques (1996) *Manufacturing the Employee: Management Knowledge from the 19ᵗʰ to 21ˢᵗ Centuries.* London: SAGE.

216 Ibid., 146.

217 Ibid., 154, original emphasis.

218 Ibid., 191.

219 Ibid., 191.

220 Jacques (2006), op. cit.

221 Bernard Burnes and Bill Cooke (2012) "The Past, Future and Present of Organization Development: Taking the Long View", *Human Relations*, 65(11) 1395–1429.

222 Bill Cooke (1999) "Writing the Left out of Management Theory: The Historiography of the Management of Change", *Management Learning*, 6/1, 81-105.

223 Ibid., 83.

224 Tomasz Ochinowski and Michał Szukała (2015) "W kierunku 'prowincjonalizacji' historii biznesu: Amerykańskie źródła a polskie doświadczenia na przykładzie propozycji interpretacyjnych prac Ryszarda Kołodziejczyka", *Klio Polska*, 7, 142-67.

225 Tomasz Ochinowski (2013) *Tradycje przedsiębiorczości w Polsce jako źródło kapitału kulturowego organizacji.* Warszawa: WZUW.

226 Monika Kostera (2012) *Organizations and Archetypes.* Cheltenham: Edward Elgar.

227 Ernst Cassirer (1946) *Language and Myth.* New York: Dover.

228 Roland Barthes (1973) *Mythologies.* London: Paladin.

229 Joseph Campbell (1988) *Myths to Live By: How We Recreate Ancient Legends in Our Daily Lives to Release Human Potential.* New York: Bantam Books, 24.

230 Joseph Campbell (1988) *The Inner Reaches of Outer Space: Metaphor as Myth and as Religion.* New York: Harper & Row.

231 Karen Armstrong (2006) *A Short History of Myth.* Edinburgh: Canongate.

232 Joseph Campbell (2004) *Pathways to Bliss: Mythology and Personal*

Transformation. Novato: New World Library.

233 Carl Gustav Jung (1990) *The Archetypes and the Collective Unconscious.* (Collected Works, Vol. 9) Princeton University Press.

234 Ibid., 32-3.

235 Martin L. Bowles (1993) "The Gods and Goddesses: Personifying Social Life in the Age of Organization", *Organization Studies,* 14/3, 395-418.

236 Martin Bowles (1991) "The Organization Shadow", *Organization Studies,* 12/3, 387-404.

237 Yiannis Gabriel (2012) "Organization in a State of Darkness: Towards a Theory of Organizational Miasma", *Organization Studies,* 33(9) 1137-52.

238 Ibid., 1141.

239 Kostera (2012), op. cit.

240 Ibid., 35.

241 Monika Kostera (2008) "The Mythologization of Organization", in: Monika Kostera (ed.) Organizational Epics and Sagas: Tales of Organizations, London: Palgrave-Macmillan, 9-13.

242 Burkard Sievers (1994) *Work, Death and Life Itself: Essays on Management and Organization.* Berlin: De Gruyter.

243 Story published originally in Kostera (2012), op. cit., 253-4.

244 Kristin Falck Saughau holds a Ph.D., MA in Theology, and is Pastor in The Danish Lutheran Church. She wrote this short reflection for this book, on my request.

245 Clifford Geertz (1993) *The Interpretation of Cultures: Selected Essays.* London: Fontana Press, emphasis subtracted, 90.

246 Karen Armstrong (2010) *The Case for God: What Religion Really Means.* London: Vintage, 4.

247 Ibid., 17.

248 Karen Armstrong (1993) *A History of God: From Abraham to the Present: The 4000-Year Quest for God.* London: Mandarin, 256.

249 William James (2008) *The Varieties of Religious Experience.* London: Routledge, 21.

250 Richard Rohr (1999) *Everything Belongs: The Gift of Contemplative*

Prayer. New York: The Crossroad Publishing Company, 31.

251 *Dhammapada,* as cited in: Jack Kornfield, (2007), *Teachings of the Buddha.* Boston: Shambala, 1.

252 Alan W. Watts (1951) *The Wisdom of Insecurity.* New York: Vintage Books.

253 Ibid., 116.

254 Jeremiah Myriam Shryock, CFR (2014) *Letters of Hope and Consolation.* San Bernardino: CFR.

255 Ibid., 2.

256 Emma Bell and Scott Taylor (2003) "The Elevation of Work: Pastoral Power and the New Age Work Ethic", *Organization,* 10/2, 329-49.

257 Ibid., 339.

258 Ibid., 330.

259 Peter Case, Robert French and Peter Simpson (2012) "From theoria to theory: Leadership without Contemplation", *Organization,* 19(3) 345-61.

260 Ibid., 345.

261 Ibid., 356.

262 Harro Höpfl (2007) "A Catholic work ethic?", *Journal of Management, Spirituality & Religion,* 4:4, 398-417.

263 Ibid., 414.

264 Miguel Pina e Cunha, Stewart R. Clegg, Cláudia Costa, António Pinto Leite, Arménio Rego, Ace Volkmann Simpson, Marta Oom de Sousa & Milton Sousa (2017) "Gemeinschaft in the midst of Gesellschaft? Love as an organizational virtue", *Journal of Management, Spirituality & Religion,* 14:1, 3-21.

265 Ibid., 12.

266 Ibid., 15.

267 Avi Kay (2012) "Pursuing Justice: Workplace Relations in the Eyes of Jewish Tradition", *Journal of Management Development,* 31/9, 901-11.

268 Laurent Gheeraert (2014) "Does Islamic Finance Spur Banking Sector Development?", *Journal of Economic Behavior & Organization,* 103, S4-S20.

269 Christine Mallin, Hisham Farag and Kean Ow-Yong (2014) "Corporate Social Responsibility and Financial Performance in Islamic Banks", *Journal of Economic Behavior & Organization,* 103, S21-S38.

270 Ronald E. Purser (2012) "Deconstructing Lack: A Buddhist Perspective on Egocentric Organizations", *Tamara Journal of Critical Inquiry,* 10/4, 17-27.

271 Ibid., 20.

272 Ronald E. Purser and Joseph Milillo (2015) "Mindfulness Revisited: A Buddhist-based Conceptualization", *Journal of Management Inquiry,* 24(1) 3–24.

273 Albert Low and Ronald Purser (2012) "Zen and the Creative Management of Dilemmas", *Journal of Management, Spirituality & Religion,* 9:4, 335–55.

274 Aminu Mamman and Hamza B. Zakaria (2016) "Spirituality and Ubuntu as the Foundation for Building African Institutions, Organizations and Leaders", *Journal of Management, Spirituality & Religion,* 13:3, 246-65.

275 Ibid., 247.

276 Pope Francis (26 April 2017) *TED talk,* https://www.ted.com/talks/pope_francis_why_the_only_future_worth_building_includes_everyone/transcript?language=en

277 Ibid.

278 Reuben Woolley (2019) "imagine an architecture / imagine a wall".in poetry collection *This Hall of Several Tortures.* Newton-le-Willows: Knives Forks and Spoons Pressforthcoming.

279 Vitruvius (2009) *On Architecture.* Transl. by Robert Tavernor and Richard Schofield, London: Penguin.

280 Ibid., 19.

281 John Ruskin (2011) *The Seven Lamps of Architecture.* Project Gutenberg, retrieved from https://www.gutenberg.org/files/35898/35898-h/35898-h.htm

282 Ibid., 198.

283 Le Corbusier (1988) *Towards a New Architecture.* New York: Dover

Publications.

284 Ibid., 1.

285 See e.g. Peter Blundell Jones, Doina Petrescu and Kim Trogal (2005) (eds) *Architecture and Participation*. London: Spoon Press.

286 Architecture for Humanity (2006) *Design Like You Give a Damn: Architectural Responses to Humanitarian Crises*. London: Thames and Hudson.

287 Cameron Sinclair (2006) "I hope it's a long list..." in: op cit.,31.

288 Much on this and other topics related to the dehumanization of public space can be found in Anna Minton's (2017) *Big Capital: Who is London For?* London: Penguin.

289 Krzysztof Nawratek and Kasia Nawratek (2015) "On the Frustrating Impossibility of Inclusive Architecture", In: Krzysztof Nawratek (Ed.) *Radical Inclusivity: Architecture and Urbanism*. Barcelona: DPR-Barcelona, 13–23.

290 Ibid., 14.

291 Ibid., 22.

292 Krzysztof Nawratek (2011) *City as a Political Idea*. University of Plymouth Press.

293 Constantin Petcou and Doina Petrescu (2015) "R-URBAN or How to Co-produce a Resilient City", *ephemera*, 15(1), 249-62.

294 Ibid., 259.

295 Tuomo Peltonen (2012) "Exploring Organizational Architecture and Space: A Case for Heterodox Research", *International Journal of Organizational Analysis*, 20(1), 68-81.

296 Krzysztof Nawratek (2012) *Holes in the Whole: Introduction to Urban Revolutions*. Winchester: Zero Books.

297 Ibid., 11.

298 Ibid., 51.

299 For an interesting presentation of the alliance of modernist architecture and scientific management, see e.g. Mauro F. Guillén (1997) "Scientific Management's Lost Aesthetic: Architecture, Organization and the Taylorized Beauty of the Mechanical", *Administrative Science Quarterly*, 42(4), 682-715.

300 See https://www.youtube.com/watch?v=5Jr83Z9k5Zc

301 The Brutalism Appreciation Society, https://www.facebook.com/groups/2256189436/

302 https://www.youtube.com/watch?v=MwC5Yer-2B0

303 Ibid.

304 Ibid.

305 http://www.mandypayneart.co.uk/

306 https://www.eventbrite.co.uk/e/park-hill-reimagined-film-launch-at-millennium-gallery-tickets-38728538100

307 Keith Collie, David Levitt and Jeremy Till (2012) *Park Hill Sheffield in Black and White*. Herne Bay: Categorical Books.

308 Ibid., 30.

309 Ibid., 30.

310 The Brutalism Appreciation Society, https://www.facebook.com/groups/2256189436/

311 Ibid.

312 Jean-Jacques Rousseau (1984) *A Discourse on Inequality*. London: Penguin.

313 Frederick Engels (2017) edited by Sankar Srinivasan, *Ludwig Feuerbach and the End of Classical German Philosophy*. India: LeoPard Books.

314 Karl Marx (1867) *Capital: Critique of the Political Economy. Book One: The Process of Production of Capital*. Marx/Engels Internet Archive (marxists.org) 1995, 1999; https://www.marxists.org/archive/marx/works/1867-c1/index.htm

315 Noam Chomsky (2012) *Occupy*. London: Penguin.

316 See *The Public Interest Sheffield Blog*; *Public Interest* at https://www.facebook.com/The.Public.Interest.Nigel.Slack/ ; Twitter Profile – @SheffCityNigel

317 Maria Daskalaki and George Kokkinidis (2017) "Organizing Solidarity Initiatives: A Socio-spatial Conceptualization of Resistance", *Organization Studies,* 38(9), 303-25.

318 Ibid., 1304.

319 Eloise Helena Livramento Dellangelo, Steffen Böhm and Patrícia

Maria Emerenciano de Mendonça (2014) "Organizing Resistance Movements: The Contribution of Political Discourse Theory", *Revista de Administração de Empresas*.

320 Thomas Swann and Konstantin Stoborod (2014) "Did you Hear the One about the Anarchist Manager?", *ephemera*, 14(4), 591-609.

321 Ibid., 599.

322 Carl Rhodes (2014) "Ethical Anarchism, Business Ethics and the Politics of Disturbance", *ephemera*, 14(4), 727-37.

323 Ibid., 727.

324 Marcelo Vieta (2014) "The Stream of Self-determination and *autogestión*: Prefiguring Alternative Economic Realities", *ephemera*, 14(4), 781-809.

325 Ibid., 784.

326 Ibid., 797.

327 Ibid., 801.

328 Monika Kostera (2014) *Occupy Management! Ideas and Inspirations for Self-management and Self-organization.* London: Routledge; and second revised edition Monika Kostera (2019) *Organize Ourselves! Inspirations and Ideas for Self-management and Self-organization.* London: MayFlyBooks/Ephemera.

329 Maria Daskalaki, email interview 2018.

330 David Ost (1991) *Solidarity and the Politics of Anti-politics: Opposition and Reform in Poland since 1968.* Philadelphia: Temple University Press.

331 Martin Parker (2008) "If Only Business Schools Wouldn't Teach Business", *The Guardian*, retrieved from https://www.theguardian.com/business/2008/nov/30/management-business-schools-capitalism-comment

332 Elton Mayo (1945) *The Social Problems of an Industrial Civilization.* New Hampshire: Ayer.

333 William Foote Whyte (1993) *Street Corner Society: The Social Structure of an Italian Slum.* Chicago: Chicago University Press.

334 Erving Goffman (1991) *Asylums: Essays on the Social Situation of Mental Patients and other Inmates.* London: Penguin.

335 Ibid., 11.

336 Ibid., 280.

337 Ibid., 265.

338 Name changed.

339 Kostera (2014), op. cit.

340 See e.g. https://www.theguardian.com/world/2018/apr/17/poland-violated-eu-laws-by-logging-in-biaowieza-forest-says-ecj

341 Martin Parker (2011) *Alternative Business: Outlaws, Crime and Culture*. Oxford: Routledge.

342 Ibid., 30.

343 Ewa Bogacz-Wojtanowska (2013) *Zdolności organizacyjne a współdziałanie organizacji pozarządowych*. Kraków: Wydawnictwo ISP UJ.

344 Maria Daskalaki (2017) "Alternative Organizing in Times of Crisis: Resistance Assemblages and Socio-spatial Solidarity", *European Urban and Regional Studies*, 1-16, https://doi.org/10.1177/096977641668300

345 Ibid., 13.

346 Zofia Łapniewska (2017) "(Re)claiming Space by Urban Commons", *Review of Radical Political Economics*, 49(1), 54-66.

347 https://occupythekitchen.org/going-in-depth-the-project

348 Kostera (2014), op. cit.

349 My language editing, edited for grammar not contents.

350 Jerzy Kociatkiewicz, Monika Kostera and Martin Parker (in review) "Tales of Disalienated Work: Learning from Alternative Organizations".

351 Peter Fleming (2017) *The Death of Homo Economicus: Work Debt and the Myth of Endless Accumulation*. London: Pluto.

352 Peter Fleming (2014) *Resisting Work: The Corporatization of Life and its Discontents*. Philadelphia: Temple University Press, 3.

353 Karl Marx (1978) "Alienation and Social Classes", in: R.C. Tucker (Ed.) *The Marx-Engels Reader*. New York: Norton, 133–5.

354 Michael Pratt (2000) "Building an Ideological Fortress: The Role of Spirituality, Encapsulation and Sense Making". *Studies in Cultures,*

Organizations and Societies, 6/1, 35-70.

355 Martin Parker (2017) "Alternative Enterprises, Local Economies and Social Justice: Why Smaller is Still More Beautiful", *M@an@ gement*, 20/4, 418-34.

356 Ibid., 418.

357 William Butler Yeats (1921) "The second coming", *Michael Robartes and the Dancer*, retrieved from http://www.theotherpages.org/poems/yeats02.html

358 E.g. Andrzej K. Koźmiński and Krzysztof Obłój (1989) *Zarys teorii równowagi organizacyjnej*. Warszawa: PWE, for a more contemporary approach, incorporating some of the insights from the cultural turn in organization studies.

359 Bauman (2017), op. cit.

360 Zygmunt Bauman (2011) *Collateral Damage: Social Inequalities in a Global Age*. Cambridge-Malden: Polity Press.

361 Ha-Joon Chang (2008) *Bad Samaritans: The Guilty Secrets of Rich Nations and the Threat to Global Prosperity*. London: Random House; Tooze (2018), op. cit.

362 Krzysztof Obłój (1986) *Zarządzanie: Ujęcie praktyczne*. Warszawa, PWE, presents the then decaying system of state communism in Poland as running in repeating negative loops, applying "more of the same" to problems and thus undermining itself. Such management, concludes the author, is deadly.

363 Humberto R. Maturana and Francisco J. Varela (1980) *Autopoiesis and Cognition: The Realization of the Living*. Holland: Reidel.

364 Antonio Gramsci (1971) *Selections from the Prison Notebooks*. (ed. Quintin Hoare and Geoffrey Nowell Smith) London: Lawrence & Wishart.

365 See e.g. Achilleas Karayiannis and Monika Kostera (2019) "The Inspirations of Heather Höpfl: Taking Heart from Radical Humanism" in Robert McMurray and Alison Pullen (eds) *Beyond Rationality in Organization and Management*. London: Routledge.

366 Armstrong (2010), op. cit.

367 Walter Benjamin (2005) *On the Concept of History*. Retrieved from

https://www.marxists.org/reference/archive/benjamin/1940/history.htm

368 Anthrakia (Monika Kostera) (2019), op. cit.

CULTURE, SOCIETY & POLITICS

The modern world is at an impasse. Disasters scroll across our smartphone screens and we're invited to like, follow or upvote, but critical thinking is harder and harder to find. Rather than connecting us in common struggle and debate, the internet has sped up and deepened a long-standing process of alienation and atomization. Zer0 Books wants to work against this trend. With critical theory as our jumping off point, we aim to publish books that make our readers uncomfortable. We want to move beyond received opinions.

Zer0 Books is on the left and wants to reinvent the left. We are sick of the injustice, the suffering, and the stupidity that defines both our political and cultural world, and we aim to find a new foundation for a new struggle.

If this book has helped you to clarify an idea, solve a problem or extend your knowledge, you may want to check out our online content as well. Look for Zer0 Books: Advancing Conversations in the iTunes directory and for our Zer0 Books YouTube channel.

Popular videos include:

Žižek and the Double Blackmain

The Intellectual Dark Web is a Bad Sign

Can there be an Anti-SJW Left?

Answering Jordan Peterson on Marxism

Follow us on Facebook
at https://www.facebook.com/ZeroBooks and Twitter at https://twitter.com/Zer0Books

Bestsellers from Zer0 Books include:

Give Them An Argument
Logic for the Left
Ben Burgis
Many serious leftists have learned to distrust talk of logic. This is
a serious mistake.
Paperback: 978-1-78904-210-8 ebook: 978-1-78904-211-5

Poor but Sexy
Culture Clashes in Europe East and West
Agata Pyzik
How the East stayed East and the West stayed West.
Paperback: 978-1-78099-394-2 ebook: 978-1-78099-395-9

An Anthropology of Nothing in Particular
Martin Demant Frederiksen
A journey into the social lives of meaninglessness.
Paperback: 978-1-78535-699-5 ebook: 978-1-78535-700-8

Cartographies of the Absolute
Alberto Toscano, Jeff Kinkle
An aesthetics of the economy for the twenty-first century.
Paperback: 978-1-78099-275-4 ebook: 978-1-78279-973-3

Malign Velocities
Accelerationism and Capitalism
Benjamin Noys
Long listed for the Bread and Roses Prize 2015, *Malign Velocities*
argues against the need for speed, tracking acceleration
as the symptom of the ongoing crises of capitalism.
Paperback: 978-1-78279-300-7 ebook: 978-1-78279-299-4

Meat Market
Female Flesh under Capitalism
Laurie Penny
A feminist dissection of women's bodies as the fleshy fulcrum of
capitalist cannibalism, whereby women are both consumers and
consumed.
Paperback: 978-1-84694-521-2 ebook: 978-1-84694-782-7

Babbling Corpse
Vaporwave and the Commodification of Ghosts
Grafton Tanner
Paperback: 978-1-78279-759-3 ebook: 978-1-78279-760-9

New Work New Culture
Work we want and a culture that strengthens us
Frithjoff Bergmann
A serious alternative for mankind and the planet.
Paperback: 978-1-78904-064-7 ebook: 978-1-78904-065-4

Romeo and Juliet in Palestine
Teaching Under Occupation
Tom Sperlinger
Life in the West Bank, the nature of pedagogy and the role of a
university under occupation.
Paperback: 978-1-78279-637-4 ebook: 978-1-78279-636-7

Ghosts of My Life
Writings on Depression, Hauntology and Lost Futures
Mark Fisher
Paperback: 978-1-78099-226-6 ebook: 978-1-78279-624-4

Sweetening the Pill
or How We Got Hooked on Hormonal Birth Control
Holly Grigg-Spall
Has contraception liberated or oppressed women?
Sweetening the Pill breaks the silence on the dark side of hormonal
contraception.
Paperback: 978-1-78099-607-3 ebook: 978-1-78099-608-0

Why Are We The Good Guys?
Reclaiming your Mind from the Delusions of Propaganda
David Cromwell
A provocative challenge to the standard ideology that Western
power is a benevolent force in the world.
Paperback: 978-1-78099-365-2 ebook: 978-1-78099-366-9

The Writing on the Wall
On the Decomposition of Capitalism and its Critics
Anselm Jappe, Alastair Hemmens
A new approach to the meaning of social emancipation.
Paperback: 978-1-78535-581-3 ebook: 978-1-78535-582-0

Enjoying It
Candy Crush and Capitalism
Alfie Bown
A study of enjoyment and of the enjoyment of studying. Bown
asks what enjoyment says about us and what we say about
enjoyment, and why.
Paperback: 978-1-78535-155-6 ebook: 978-1-78535-156-3

Color, Facture, Art and Design
Iona Singh
This materialist definition of fine-art develops guidelines for
architecture, design, cultural-studies and ultimately social
change.
Paperback: 978-1-78099-629-5 ebook: 978-1-78099-630-1

Neglected or Misunderstood
The Radical Feminism of Shulamith Firestone
Victoria Margree
An interrogation of issues surrounding gender, biology,
sexuality, work and technology, and the ways in which our
imaginations continue to be in thrall to ideologies of maternity
and the nuclear family.
Paperback: 978-1-78535-539-4 ebook: 978-1-78535-540-0

How to Dismantle the NHS in 10 Easy Steps (Second Edition)
Youssef El-Gingihy
The story of how your NHS was sold off and why you will have
to buy private health insurance soon. A new expanded second
edition with chapters on junior doctors' strikes and government
blueprints for US-style healthcare.
Paperback: 978-1-78904-178-1 ebook: 978-1-78904-179-8

Digesting Recipes
The Art of Culinary Notation
Susannah Worth
A recipe is an instruction, the imperative tone of the expert, but this constraint can offer its own kind of potential. A recipe need not be a domestic trap but might instead offer escape – something to fantasise about or aspire to.

Paperback: 978-1-78279-860-6 ebook: 978-1-78279-859-0

Most titles are published in paperback and as an ebook. Paperbacks are available in traditional bookshops. Both print and ebook formats are available online.
Follow us on Facebook
at https://www.facebook.com/ZeroBooks
and Twitter at https://twitter.com/Zer0Books